Classic Diners of CONNECTICUT

GARRISON LEYKAM

Forewords by LARRY CULTRERA & CHRISTOPHER DOBBS

AMERICAN PALATE

Published by American Palate
A Division of The History Press
Charleston, SC 29403
www.historypress.net

Bottom cover photo by David M. Williams.

All images are from the author's collection.

First published 2013

Manufactured in the United States

ISBN 978.1.62619.215.7

Library of Congress CIP data applied for.

Contents

Foreword, by Larry Cultrera   5
Foreword, by Christopher Dobbs   7
Preface   11
Acknowledgements   17

A Short-Order History of Diners   21
Counter Culture   29
Fairfield County   33
New Haven County   58
Hartford County   76
Middlesex County   100
Litchfield County   106
New London County   113
Windham County   121
Classic Diners of Connecticut Past   126

Appendix I: Diner Lingo   135
Appendix II: Diner Recipes   151
Appendix III: Connecticut Diner Directory by Manufacturer   161
Index   167
About the Author   171

Foreword

There are many people who consider the phrase "classic diner" to mean only those factory-built restaurants that resemble railroad cars manufactured from the 1920s through the 1950s. I personally believe that because diners have always evolved and changed with the times, the term "classic" should encompass every style of diner that came along—from the horse-drawn lunch wagons of the late 1800s to the multi-sectioned diner-restaurants that seat upward of two hundred people (or more) still being built in the year 2013.

The state of Connecticut is home to many diners. In fact, it has more modern diners (diners built after the year 1960) than any other New England state.

My interest in the American diner started when I was very young, probably around the age of four or five. I always noticed roadside businesses and buildings, using them as landmarks. Diners were an early fascination, given that there were many of them in the metropolitan Boston area during the 1950s and 1960s. By the end of the 1970s, I had a growing awareness through my travels around northern New England that this truly American institution known as the diner had been noticeably disappearing from cities and towns and along the roadsides as the years had passed.

In April 1979, I had begun a journey, embarking on what I ultimately referred to as a personal research project that basically started right after I bought my very first brand-new vehicle, a bright blue Chevy van. Toward the end of 1979, I started to go out on Sunday morning rides with a pal, Steve Repucci. We made a conscious decision to go to local diners for breakfast.

By mid-1980, I had purchased a used 35mm camera, which led me into taking a very tentative first photograph of the Bypass Diner in Harrisburg, Pennsylvania, on November 29, 1980. Since that time, I have managed to document more than 830 diners with my photographs.

I was contacted in early 2011 about the possibility of authoring a book. This became *Classic Diners of Massachusetts* (published in October 2011) and was the first of a new series for The History Press that would be followed by *The History of Diners in New Jersey* (Michael Gabriele, 2013) and this book, *Classic Diners of Connecticut*, by Garrison Leykam (also in 2013).

With all the diner buff/enthusiasts I have met over the years, I have learned that like the people themselves, the reasons they love diners are varied. Some of these enthusiasts, like me, have memories from their youth usually revolving around family road trips or just Saturday or Sunday breakfasts at their local neighborhood diner with their family. Garrison Leykam is one of those people and has had similar memories that little by little became ingrained into his psyche, and he has carried that love into the next generation with a tradition he has passed on to his son and daughter.

After our initial contact, I eventually got to be interviewed for one of the Saturday morning *Those Diner and Motorcycle Guys* shows that aired on March 16, 2013. Garrison and I also met face to face for breakfast one Sunday morning a month later at Kelly's Diner in Somerville, Massachusetts. We found that we are truly kindred spirits, and even though we both have traveled somewhat different paths in our life, there has always been a common denominator: the diner. Garrison's love of the American diner is evident, and it comes through in his interesting style of writing. Through his interviewing skills, he lets the respective diner owner's own words tell the story. He has included recipes from several of the featured diners, as well as a section on the old "diner lingo," a form of shorthand that was used for ordering food that some countermen and waitresses used back in the 1940s and 1950s.

So, sit back and relax (try not to get too hungry, I dare you) and enjoy *Classic Diners of Connecticut*!

Larry Cultrera
Saugus, Massachusetts

Foreword

G arrison Leykam has created a long-overdue book by writing *Classic Diners of Connecticut*. Previous books have focused on the history of these all-American eateries, on New England diners or, justifiably, on those from New Jersey. Not until now has any book specifically explored the people and places of the Nutmeg State's diners. Leykam has taken the time to examine Connecticut's rich diner culture, to meet the hardworking and dedicated owners and staff who bring them to life, to enjoy a meal with other hungry patrons and to document the uniqueness of these institutions. His enjoyment of people is matched only by his obvious passion for these gastronomic fueling stations of home-cooked delights.

Diners speak as much about our country's and state's complex cultural evolution and heritage as anything. Connecticut has provided the country such literary icons as Mark Twain and Harriet Beecher Stowe, as well as my favorite author, educator and cultural definer, Noah Webster. It has also been the home to the likes of industrialist Samuel Colt, inventor Eli Whitney and entertainment pioneer P.T. Barnum. With this heritage of ingenuity and creativity, it is no wonder that our state has played a significant role with diners. While there is some historic debate, we as proud Nutmeggers *know* that Louis Lassen invented the hamburger in about 1900 from his New Haven lunch wagon (aka Louis' Lunch). And what would the diner be without the hamburger? It is placed on the diner's epicurean pedestal with meatloaf, pancakes and bottomless coffee.

As a social historian and material culturalist, it matters less to me who actually invented the hamburger and more what its existence says about us. The hamburger and the diner provide valuable insight into American habits. As Rudyard Kipling once noted, "The American does not drink at meals as a sensible man should. Indeed, he has no meals. He stuffs for ten minutes thrice a day." I might find this offensive if I did not think it so true. What Kipling observed was the impact of the Industrial Revolution and the abiding American belief that time is money. In 1820, the United States' population was a little over 9.5 million people; by 1870, mass immigration helped swell our numbers to more than 38 million. This expansion brought about significant change as the country was transformed from a predominantly agrarian economy to one heavily concentrated in urban industrial areas. By 1870, America had also survived the bloody Civil War. Just as World War II would spark innovation and propel the country to a new level of production, so too did the Civil War. Connecticut and the rest of the Northeast played pivotal roles in this demographic and technological change. Into this restive atmosphere on an 1872 night in nearby Providence, Rhode Island, the American diner was born.

In my own research, writing and lecturing, I have focused on the "American diner" (differentiating it from that of the later Greek diner or the restaurant that calls itself a diner) as a critical piece of American material culture. From an academic perspective, I am fascinated by their architecture and cultural roles. What does it say about the ideas, people and beliefs of the society that produced and ate in diners?

Both scholars and hungry patrons have supplied four essential characteristics to the American diner:

- the structure must be prefabricated and hauled to a site;
- it must have a counter and stools;
- it should offer home-style cooking at reasonable prices;
- the cooking should take place behind a counter.

There is a fifth characteristic that I feel has largely been neglected: the classic American diner is architecturally linked to transportation. Its development follows the evolution of transportation and our infatuation with it. The early diner manufacturers drew on the skills of the wagon maker and coach painter. Their barrel-top roofs and large wheels were designed to withstand the elements and poor roads. Specific colors and designs followed that of show- and trade-wagons. As transportation evolved, lunch wagon manufacturers sought a new and improved look. The Delmonico in 1868 was Pullman's first specially designed railroad dining car. Many of these railroad cars had monitor roofs with a transom to allow light and fresh air into the structure. They also had arched ornamental sashes with interiors of dark wood and tables running the length of the cars. By the early 1900s, manufacturers of lunch wagons had embraced these elements and the name—"diner." Skee's Diner in Torrington and North Canaan's Collin's Diner are some of the finest examples of this style.

By the mid-twentieth century, diner manufacturers needed a new look to appeal to their clients. They took elements from aviation, the automobile industry and railroads to incorporate Art Deco and aerodynamic aesthetics, as well as newer manmade products such as stainless steel, Bakelite and Connecticut's locally raised, genuine synthetic Naugahyde. Leading the charge was the flashy bullet-like train by Bud Manufacturing Company, the Burlington Zephyr. With rounded corners and speed-lines, the train heralded a new age. A 1937 Bud Company ad showing a streamlined train hurtling into a sunburst noted: "Bud designers and fabricators have looked to the future. They have taken the long view." Diner manufacturers took this view, too, by incorporating streamlining and integrating the sunburst into their back bar and other elements. Newington's Olympia Diner and Zip's in Dayville are two prime examples.

From the late 1950s through the 1960s, America was obsessed with the space race. Diner manufacturers once again adapted their image to evoke the newest transportation craze. Doorways sometimes resembled launching pads, zigzag canopies suggested stars and lighting fixtures and signs often resembled flying saucers. These cool, architecturally designed looks for a new age would have made George Jetson feel at home. The Star Diner in New Haven will take you into the Milky Way. As a side note, it also boasts on its sign "PIZZA"—another food "invented" in Connecticut that speaks to the diner as a culinary melting pot.

The space-age diner was one of the last of its kind that directly reflected transportation. Since the 1970s, the American diner has been in decline, yet its allure continues. I grew up in Ridgefield, Connecticut, in the 1980s with a World War II–generation father. He loved taking me to diners, and I quickly developed a passion for them myself. The Collin's Diner in North Canaan is one of those special places that I connect with my father and good times. Even as a teenager, I was enchanted by diners' atmospheres, good food and pleasant if at times colorful staff. In high school and college, I hung out with the guys, celebrated after pulling an all-nighter on a term paper and took girlfriends to diners like the Holiday Diner in Danbury. Now as a father, I enjoy taking my boys to such diners as O'Rourke's in Middletown and the less traditional East West Grill in West Hartford.

Classic Diners of Connecticut revs like one of Leykam's other passions—motorcycles. It takes the reader on a road trip down Connecticut's byways to explore the people and places that have helped shape an American icon. Each generation and ethnic group has left its mark on the diner. In Connecticut, you can find Indian, Irish, Thai, Greek, Polish, Italian and many other foods coming out of their kitchens. Our state's industrial and cultural history is on their walls and served up on their tables. The diner lives on as long as we remember and appreciate an institution that is as individualistic as our American soul.

Christopher Dobbs

Preface

The significance of the College Diner in my personal life goes beyond my recognition of its coveted place in the history of American classic diners. The humble eatery—located on North Avenue in New Rochelle, New York, across the street from Iona College from which it derived its name—symbolizes for me the transition from perpetually moving army brat to community-based family member. Amid the smell of home cooking, the smiling faces of the familiar patrons and the art of spontaneous conversation, I was served a lifetime portion of acceptance and socialization from which I continue to savor the leftovers.

I was born in 1949 at Alexandria Hospital in northern Virginia, formerly the Alexandria Infirmary Association, formed in 1872 and the first hospital to staff its emergency department with full-time physicians twenty-four hours a day. My father, John Edward Leykam, was stationed at the time at nearby Fort Belvoir, founded during World War I as Camp A.A. Humphreys and renamed in the 1930s in recognition of the Belvoir plantation that once occupied the site. The post was originally the home of the Army Engineer School prior to its relocation in the 1980s to Fort Leonard Wood, in Missouri. With roots in his hometown of Brooklyn, my father was determined to one day return north. It wasn't long before the Leykam family's Ford Super DeLuxe station wagon was taking us to my father's new assignment at the U.S. Army garrison at Fort Hamilton. A major embarkation center during both world wars, our time at Fort Hamilton was appropriately short-lived, as my father's gypsy-like propensity for being constantly on the move outweighed his original motivation simply to relocate.

Like a collective "Where's Waldo?" once again the Leykam personnel and associated stores were loaded into the car, and we headed to Fort Totten in Bayside, Queens. Originally constructed to protect the East River approach to New York Harbor, the fort became a Project Nike air defense site in 1954, although no missiles were ever located there except for the unarmed one that was part of the "Welcome to Fort Totten" sign that greeted visitors when they entered. My father's assignment at Fort Totten was discontinued by him years before the post's 1974 closing and conversion to a public park, with its Visitor's Center morphing into a museum with exhibits about the history of Fort Totten. My father had decommissioned the Ford in favor of a 1952 Chevrolet Styleline four-door sedan that I think was meant by him to herald yet another move in my first four years of life as a new beginning. And, in fact, this move would prove to be exactly that as we crossed the Throgs Neck Bridge into Westchester County.

My father remained in the service but relinquished his noncommissioned officer status and took a civilian personnel position at Fort Slocum, New York, a military base that occupied Davids' Island on the western end of Long Island Sound in New Rochelle, New York. Military use of the island goes back to 1862, when the United States government leased the land and installed the De Camp General Hospital to treat thousands of wounded soldiers from the battlefields of the American Civil War. Davids' Island evolved into a principal depot of the U.S. Army General Recruiting Service as thousands of recruits made the ferry ride to the island sign-up post. Davids' Island was renamed Fort Slocum upon its conversion to a coastal artillery defense post, adding twenty new brick buildings, including officers' quarters, enlisted men's barracks, mess halls, hospital buildings and support facilities. Fort Slocum became the home of the U.S. Army Chaplain School and the site of the U.S. Army Information School offering training in journalism, public affairs and photography.

For the Leykam family, the relocation to New Rochelle meant no more transient living in military housing. We had our first real home on Brookside Place, where I would grow up, attend Holy Family School and play stickball in the streets with sewer plates as first and third bases. Front-porch neighbors would obligingly move their cars to extend the ball field, as well as to protect their windshields. I would learn to play the guitar, form a band, attend Iona Prep with fellow alumnus and former chairman and CEO of Sony Music Tommy Mottola, play the same college coffeehouse circuit as fellow Iona

College student and "American Pie" songwriter Don McLean and open for the Beach Boys and the Four Tops on the steps of Spellman Hall.

However, living in the "Queen City of the Sound," the inspiration for George M. Cohan's song "Forty-five Minutes from Broadway" and the fictional home of Rob and Laura Petrie, came at a price. In order to afford our first home, my father took a full-time human resources position at New Rochelle Hospital and worked evenings and Saturdays at Schindel's Army & Navy store. My mother took an administrative position at Iona College to add income to the family till and to take advantage of the employee benefits package to help make her dream of seeing my brother, John, and me get a college education, which neither of my parents had. She worked evenings at the Pam Clock Company fulfilling orders for its aluminum, metal and glass backlit advertising clocks featured in advertisements for companies like Coca-Cola.

To make the dream of homeownership possible meant that much of our family interaction was of the "ships passing in the night" kind, with hellos and goodbyes separated by increasingly diminished quality time and my parents supporting a platoon of sitters for my brother and me. Except for Sundays. Sunday was family time together, and the morning always began with breakfast at the College Diner. Even the family car was given a respite from the frenetic pace of the six-day workweek and the disconnectedness accompanying it. In military style reminiscent of his days as a technical sergeant, my father would have us all "fall in" for dress inspection on the front porch, and then he would lead our walk up Brookside Place with his trademark stiff wave to the neighbors along the way. At the top of the street, we would make a suggestive military parade "dress right" at the Dino the Dinosaur sign at the Sinclair gas station onto North Avenue for the few blocks' walk to the College Diner.

We were family and proud of it. And as we entered the diner, we felt socially embraced by the extended family of patrons with their smiling faces, the "how've you been?" inquiries and their "kids are sure getting big" observations. The owner, Don Zappavigna, would greet my father with a strong handshake and approving pat on the back as he led us, menus in hand, to a vacant booth. I often lagged behind, fascinated as I always was by the grill cook behind the counter orchestrating a symphony of eggs, home fries, bacon, sausage and pancakes conducted according to the sheet music of guest checks hanging from the hood vent. I was mesmerized, interrupted only by my father calling me from across the diner to join the rest of the family. To this day, I cannot help but be moved by Norman Rockwell's 1958 painting *The Runaway*, which depicts a young boy sitting with a protective highway patrolman at the counter of a diner. Rockwell's brushstrokes capture the feeling of belongingness over isolation that is integral to the diner experience, as well as my own. Being an army brat meant changing schools, moving to different neighborhoods and making new friends—all things that contributed to a sense of disconnectedness and transience. The College Diner gave me the earliest feelings of "belonging" that I can remember.

Sundays at the College Diner symbolize for me the essence of classic diners—the closest relationship between eating out and eating at home that exists. It's linear-culinary convergence. Like the railroad tracks that appear to meet the closer they get to the horizon, the sense of family that develops between diner staff and patrons becomes one's extended family. Good food, friendly conversation and a genuine regard for one another's welfare epitomize the true diner. The intellectual pursuit of asking, "What is a true diner?" has spawned a platoon of researchers and writers who have amassed a rich historical data pool of architectural and manufacturing information about diners that we can all draw from to enhance our own anecdotal experiences. However, for me, the litmus test of what is the best answer to "What is a true diner?" is the very personal experience that one has being in a diner. It's not part of the architectural design or building as created by the manufacturer. The diner experience comes from within and is drawn outward from the core of who we are by the sights, smells and sounds around us. It's within the diner that we find ourselves.

I've cherished my College Diner experiences throughout my life, taking every opportunity to bring my son, Christopher, and my daughter, Morgan, to diners as part of our family time together. We would play a game whereby all clocks would stop when we sat down in the booth, and we had to talk only in the present tense—about what were we thinking, what were we feeling and what was important to share with one another. Anytime someone talked about the past or the future, they were penalized a French fry or some other savored food item—with young kids, this can get very territorial! Enjoying wonderful home-cooked food together and simply "being" with one another made our diner time stand out from the busy-ness and distractions of the "normal" week.

I had the opportunity to take my love of classic diners to another level by producing and hosting the *DINERS* TV show on Connecticut Public Television (CPTV). Open casting calls were held at motorcycle dealerships during which prospective riders were asked to describe their passions for diners and motorcycles and to demonstrate any unique talents they had that would convince me to choose them to accompany me on my chrome and neon adventures. Through surprise twists in the road, candid interviews and audition clips, viewers found that their stereotypical image of who rides motorcycles today was given an extreme makeover. The reward at the end of the ride was a celebratory meal at a classic diner. Don Clady, editor of *Connecticut Cruise News* and producer of the *Super Sunday* motorcycle show, wrote, "Of all the motorcycle and food shows out there, *DINERS* is the most accurate portrayal I've seen about who today's bikers are and the classic diners they frequent."

Custom motorcycle builder Cyril Huze summed up the relationship between motorcycles and diners, saying, "Like burgers and ketchup, bikes and diners mix very well with each other…[it's all about] the joy of being on a motorcycle and finding those out-of-the-way classic eateries that invite travelers in for a home-cooked meal and friendly conversation while transporting them back in time." Even the governor of Connecticut, M. Jodi Rell, shared her excitement about the *DINERS* motorcycle: "It is my pleasure to offer my most sincere congratulations to you on the occasion of the *DINERS* motorcycle appearing in the Motorcycle Hall of Fame Museum's 'MotoStars: Celebrities + Motorcycles' exhibit. I commend and congratulate the talented individuals who have dedicated their time and effort into the creation of this magnificent motorcycle. I am proud to join you and the rest of Connecticut as your work is rewarded with the honor of being included in the Motorcycle Hall of Fame's exhibit."

My passion for classic diners and my involvement in the media led me to produce and host the radio program *Those Diner and Motorcycle Guys* with cohost Ralph DeLuco; in its first year online, it has garnered well over 1 million listeners around the world. The interview-format show taps a varied roster of guests from film, music and TV, as well as manufacturers, journalists and adventurers who share my passion for classic diners, motorcycles and life on the road.

This book is intended for the dedicated diner enthusiast, as well as those who want an introduction to what I believe are the best representations of classic diners in the Nutmeg State. It fits easily into a glove compartment or motorcycle saddlebag, and for ease of reference, I've organized the contents by county. Each section highlights those diners that meet my criteria for "classic," reminiscent of my own experiences as to what truly makes a diner a diner. I've incorporated excerpts from interviews I've conducted with diner owners, as I believe they give insight into that infamous question better than anyone else can. I have included information of a historical and manufacturing nature as to each diner, but I have been vigilant to make sure that the diner "experience" is told from the perspective of the owners themselves and their stories of entrepreneurism, immigration, adapting to a challenging economy, responding to a competitive chain restaurant landscape, determination, hard work, putting the customer first and caring for their patrons beyond the diner walls. I've also included some diner recipes to whet your appetite for visiting the contributing diners and tasting the real thing. There is a chapter on "diner lingo" to give you the inside edge on classic diner vernacular, an introduction to the diner-specific "counter culture" and recognition for diners in Connecticut no longer operationally with us but whose presence on the eternal roadways of life remain socially and culturally significant.

Disclaimer: We currently live in a fragile economy that affects small business decision-making, so certain information contained in Classic Diners of Connecticut *is subject to change, such as operating hours, menu items, pricing and, sadly, even a diner's very existence. I have diligently avoided including information that could vary as time marches on, but given the nature of the diner business, some content may unavoidably change.*

Acknowledgements

Frequenting diners as often as I do, I couldn't begin to quantify the number of occasions when I sat in a diner booth, looking over all of the wonderful selections on the menu, and commented, "I don't know where to begin." Fortunately, Nanci Fox has given me the beginning of acknowledging all of the people who made *Classic Diners of Connecticut* a reality. She has made countless calls to diner owners and historians in researching this book and collecting recipes, contributing hours upon hours of work for which I am so very grateful. As an author, the gift of keeping me organized is well received and much appreciated. Nanci's motivation, support and encouragement, as well as her positive responses to the question I've asked of her time and time again—namely, "Do you want to go to a diner?"—have made writing *Classic Diners of Connecticut* an absolute pleasure. I love you for a lifetime.

Had it not been for my father, John Edward Leykam, and my mother, Rose B. Tittmann-Leykam, I most assuredly would have missed the opportunity to experience my first diner and to continue to associate with diners the values inherent in "family" and "hard work." As I wrote this book, I came to miss you both even more since I've realized the depth to which the values you have instilled in me have let me experience to the fullest those values embraced by the diner owners I've met with and interviewed. I am sure that you are both sitting at a booth in the Eternal Diner ordering from the celestial blue-plate specials. Enjoy!

Classic diners and family are synonymous, and my son, Christopher, and my daughter, Morgan, have taught an aging head of family what family is all about. Age does not always guarantee wisdom, and both of you have taught me lessons about love, caring, honesty, responsibility and communication that feel like they're as new and fresh as today's diner special. This book could not have been written authentically from the approach I took without all the wonderful lessons you have taught me. I love you both immensely. The rush of memories I experience when I visit a diner and smile to myself are those that we have shared together.

To Christopher Dobbs, executive director of the Noah Webster House and West Hartford Historical Society, who is an expert on diner architecture, you have been an inspiration by virtue of your following and sharing your passion for classic diners. Your entertaining and informative road show presentation, "Wagon Wheels and Stainless Steel: The Architecture of the American Diner," is testimony to the depth of your knowledge about diners and your educated knack for motivating others to learn more about what we know experientially and anecdotally.

Like my own diner Buddha, Larry Cultrera has been my sage in writing *Classic Diners of Connecticut*. You have been a tremendous and reliable resource in researching as well as writing this book. You had the courage to challenge me when we didn't agree while respecting my point of view when I wouldn't relinquish it. Your friendship is the ketchup to my cheeseburger. This book would not have been possible without your guidance and critiques. I value the friendship with you that has increased commensurately with the word count.

My commissioning editor, Alyssa Kate Pierce, has been my Obi-Wan Kenobi, guiding me through the labyrinthine writing journey and belaying me as an author when my footing was not secure. I have learned more than the craft of writing from you. Thanks for always being there.

To all the diner owners I had the opportunity to meet and interview in researching and writing this book, I am most appreciative for the time we spent talking. I've learned so very much from you, not only about managing and operating a diner but also about life itself, family values, the courage of entrepreneurism, caring about others and what's most important in life. I have written *Classic Diners of Connecticut* in such a way as to incorporate and preserve the philosophy of life that you all embrace and convey. Your diner stories have impressed me deeply, and I humbly hope that you find this book adequate appreciation for what you have shared.

To all the local historians, I am deeply grateful for your enthusiastic "filling in of the blanks" of the available information on diners and for providing me with a deeper local history of them. Your assistance is much appreciated, especially Marilyn Labbe, Barbara Davis, Mary Rose Deveau and Mark McEachern.

To my best friend, Rich Eisenman, you know me about as well as anyone ever has, and you are always there for me, even in my most frenetic state as an author approaching deadlines. Those diner breakfasts and lunches together and the occasional quick cup of coffee have been my salvation when times were low and my celebrations when times were great. God bless you and thank you.

To Ralph DeLuca, my cohost on our *Those Diner and Motorcycle Guys* radio program, our times at the microphone have been among my most wonderful life experiences. There's no one I'd rather talk about motorcycles and diners with than you.

To our dog, Toots, a *high paw-to-the-hand five* for lying beside me as I typed and for being my most loyal buddy. I admire your ability to wag your tail and smile that doggy type of smile, especially during those times when my verbal tirades over a frustrating point in the writing process got the better of me. You are truly man's best friend.

When the last domino goes down and the task is accomplished, one must look back to the beginning and recognize the first dominoes that put the motion in process and led the way for all of the ones that followed. In writing and completing this book, I would be remiss in not giving recognition to those pioneers in the field of diner research and authorship without whom the intellectual pursuit of putting into words what we know and love (diners) would neither be possible nor credible. Among these are Richard J.S. Gutman, Kellie O. Guttman, Donald Kaplan, Allyson Bellink, Randy Garbin and all of the passionate "diner literati" who have contributed to the growing wealth of information available on diners.

A Short-Order History of Diners

A ll successful businesses start with the identification of a need for which they offer a solution. The origin of the American diner is credited to Walter Scott, who in 1872 equipped his Providence, Rhode Island–based horse-drawn wagon to serve sandwiches, boiled eggs, pies and coffee to factory workers, notably those on the night (or third) shift, looking for a hot meal. His business took off, as measured not only by the growing number of food carts in his own fleet but also by the number of competitors who observed Scott's success and jumped on the food wagon concept with their own rolling eateries, including a Providence policeman named Ruel B. Jones, who grew his own fleet into seven carts.

The success of Walter Scott's lunch wagon fleet was spread from Rhode Island to Massachusetts by Ruel Jones's Worcester-based cousin, Samuel Messer Jones, who started out with a typical wagon from which he handed out previously prepared food to his blue-collar clientele. Jones would eventually amass enough funds within a few short years to have a completely new wagon built to his specifications that was large enough to include a cooking area. Now, not only could patrons walk up to a window on the side of Scott's cart to purchase their food and then sit curbside to eat, but the new expanded wagon also allowed another new twist: Jones made it possible for a handful of customers to actually come inside and be served. Fellow Worcester businessman Charles Palmer would ultimately buy Samuel Messer Jones's burgeoning business and patent his lunch wagon design.

As with all successful enterprises, someone comes along to take it to the next level. In this case, Worcester businessman T.H. Buckley decided that there was more money to be made by securing a patent for the design of these lunch wagons than actually operating them, and so the New England Lunch Wagon Company (later named the T.H. Buckley Lunch Wagon and Catering Company) was born to meet the growing demand for mobile lunch wagons. He added touches to his wagons that remain hallmarks of what we associate with their evolution into many of the classic diners around today, namely barrel roofs, shiny fixtures, frosted glass and ornate signage. Buckley would become referred to as the "lunch wagon king" among the fraternity of "diner-preneurs" in recognition of his being the mastermind behind the appearance of diners in 275 towns across the United States, including the flagship of mass-produced lunch wagons, the White House Cafés. Wilfred H. Barriere and Stearns A. Haynes, a carpenter and blacksmith, respectively, combined their trade skills to form a Worcester-based diner construction company that was eventually purchased by Philip H. Duprey and renamed the Worcester Lunch Car and Carriage Manufacturing Company.

New lunch wagon companies owned by Patrick J. Tierney in New Rochelle, New York, and Jerry O'Mahony in Bayonne, New Jersey, marked the next geometric and competitive leap in diner evolution as manufacturing competition came into full swing. Counters grew longer, side entrances invited those used to standing and eating under awnings inside, porcelain panels made their appearance and even that item that we take for granted today, the bathroom, became a welcome new convenience. More manufacturers appeared on the scene: Bixler, Brill, Pollard, Sterling, Wason and Ward & Dickinson. The Pullman railroad cars, the distant cousins of the horse-drawn lunch wagons, were the inspiration for additional diner styling and especially for the new "official" name for these unique eateries: "diners." Railroad dining cars were an inspiration for diner design and functionality, but this was not a literal transformation of one into the other, which is where much of the popular confusion arises as to the origin of diners.

Whereas Scott's original lunch wagon brought food to the factory workers (and assorted street urchins and night owls), Henry Ford's mass production of the automobile and Americans' instant love affair with it spawned a network of new roads and the need to satiate the growing number of hungry drivers en route to their jobs or recreation. Early curbside food stands capitalized on the quickly growing demand for "road food," and these rapidly evolved into the more thematic White Castles and White Towers.

The Depression heralded a "fix what you've got" mentality in response to the exigencies of the economy. With no available capital to build new and larger diners, companies like Kullman responded by creating the "mini" diner in response to a demand for their "dining carts." Accompanied by the availability of inexpensive but good food, these scaled-down depression-era versions of their larger counterparts flourished and reaffirmed Scott's original "bring the food to the people" success formula by literally transporting these smaller, horseless eateries on flatbeds each day to their designated sites.

In spite of the fact that the severe worldwide economic depression known as the Great Depression started in most countries in 1930 and lasted most of the decade (and in some places into the '40s), the face of the American drive-in restaurant contradicted the financial crisis underneath, although it maintained diners' connection with industrialism. Art Deco, an influential visual arts design style, first appeared in France during the 1920s and combined traditional craft motifs with Machine Age imagery and materials, mesmerizing the world with its rich colors, bold geometric shapes and lavish ornamentation. Art Deco represented rapid industrialization and its transformation of culture as Americans awakened to and embraced new technology. Drive-ins outlandishly embraced Art Deco aesthetics representing luxury, glamour, exuberance and faith in social and technological progress and blinded the reality of the Depression behind neon lighting complemented by waitresses in equally garish outfits and an expanded menu to entice customers.

Sterling-manufactured "Streamliners" built by J.B. Judkins Company of Merrimac, Massachusetts, prefigured Jetsonsian space-age design and the speed with which America was embracing technology. The new techno age was symbolized by the diner's sleek, bullet-shaped design. The growing number of in-vogue diner manufacturers, like DeRaffele, Fodero, Mountain View and Paramount, was matched by the variety of architectural diner elements, including flat-paneled porcelain terracotta (and its fluted or tubed counterpart, stainless steel), block glass and Formica. It would take the impact of World War II to bring diner outlandishness into reality, not only in terms of the menu reflecting the short supply of basic foodstuffs but also in the lack of availability of building materials and male labor, which would put a temporary halt to new diner construction. With more and more men on the front lines, women would perform the roles of waitstaff, ultimately "Flo-izing" it into a characteristically female position. Americans' new mobility was evident in the diner manufacturing process itself, with

Paramount Diners' patent for the split-construction method enabling diners to be constructed in sections and transported like giant Lego sets to their designated locations, a methodology that continues today.

Diners experienced a post–World War II manufacturing resurgence absent the overconfident gaudiness of its aesthetic predecessors as demonstrated by the abandonment of the more expensive building and outfitting materials like leather, mahogany and marble in favor of Formica, Naugahyde and steel tubing. Diner manufacturers like Comac, Manno, Master and Supreme brought about a return to practicality and with it a shifting of emphasis away from space-age design to practical operationalism.

As Americans shifted into the hyper-drive of postwar economic optimism, mass consumerism and the demand for readily available "feel good" products carried over into the restaurant business and provided the raison d'être for the proliferation of fast-food chains like McDonalds and Burger King. Whereas diners originally emerged in response to the need of working-class Americans to have access to inexpensive hot food during their factory shifts, the success of post–World War II fast-food chains fostered a culture of entitlement and laziness, fundamentally changing not only how Americans eat but also how we relate to one another. The diners' stock and trade of home-cooked meals became overshadowed by quickly prepared and readily convenient food that can be consumed at a whim without even having to leave your car. The insularity of the drive-thru window and "advantage" of never having to get out of one's car run counter to the essence of diner life: the conversation and interaction of the patrons and staff and the building of interpersonal relationships that transcend the retail exchange of food and services.

There is a resurgent interest today in classic diners that accompanies an overall trend toward retro fascination. For diner advocates like me, the interest in classic diners goes far deeper than the contemporary inclination toward repackaging restaurants with an abundance of eBay-procured '50s memorabilia and plenty of bright neon reflecting off endless stainless steel in a feigned attempt to capture the essence of the classic diner. You can't bid, buy, build or broker the "secret sauce" of a classic diner. It's there or it's not, plain and simple—just like diner food.

The Diner Manufacturers' Timeline
(by Date of Business Start)

Charles H. Palmer, Worcester, Massachusetts, 1889–1901. It was the first to receive a patent for his design for a night lunch wagon and one of the earliest successful lunch wagon builders. The company came to an end in 1901 when fire destroyed his factory in Sterling Junction, Massachusetts.

New England Lunch Wagon Company (later named the T.H. Buckley Lunch Wagon and Catering Company), Worcester, Massachusetts, 1891–1908. Thomas H. Buckley became the first "lunch wagon king," setting up lunch wagons in 275 towns throughout the country.

Wilfred H. Barriere, Worcester, Massachusetts, 1905–6 and 1926–36. It was noted for the varying sizes of its diners.

Worcester Lunch Car Company, Worcester, Massachusetts, 1906–61. It was noted for the craftsmanship of its small, handcrafted diner with porcelain exterior and hardwood interior, Gothic lettering painted on the porcelain front panels and colorfully striped awnings; built more than six hundred diners.

John J.E. Hennigan, Worcester, Massachusetts, 1907–17. Hennigan was a night lunch wagon operator turned manufacturer; the company produced a model known as the Franklin Lunch Wagon.

Jerry O'Mahony Inc., Elizabeth, New Jersey, 1913–56. A leader in diner production for several decades, it introduced stainless steel exteriors in the late 1940s and produced several large double-unit diners. Many classic diners from the '40s and '50s that survive to this day were built by O'Mahony.

Mulholland Company, Dunkirk, New York, 1920–30. Founded as the Mulholland Spring Company in 1881, the company built buggies, carriages and road wagons, advancing to automobile, truck and ambulance bodies and later manufacturing diners in 1920.

Ward & Dickinson, Silver Creek, New York, 1923–40. It built a distinctive diner based on the designs of railroad or trolley cars; it was the most prolific of the diner builders in the Lake Erie region of New York State.

The Pollard Company, Lowell, Massachusetts, 1926–27. It built a handful of barrel-roofed diners.

Kullman Industries Inc., Avenel, New Jersey, 1927–2011. It was a builder of space age–style diners; it was founded by Samuel Kullman, the former accountant for P.J. Tierney Sons.

J.G. Brill Company, Dining Car Division, Philadelphia, Pennsylvania, 1927–32. It was a noted manufacturer of street railway vehicles that diversified by introducing a line of all-steel diners.

Silk City Diners (Paterson Vehicle Company), Paterson, New Jersey, 1927–64. Having started as a wagon builder, it was characterized by its fine craftsmanship across a variety of diner styles; it also featured a combination of stainless steel and porcelain in many different color schemes, with the diner's name displayed on a large horizontal porcelain stripe. These were the lowest-priced diners you could buy at the time.

Bixler Manufacturing Company, Norwalk, Ohio, 1931–37. Bixler diners featured extreme width for the period, two-foot double-hung windows and a barrel roof with a fancy profile on the ends.

Paramount Diners, Oakland, New Jersey, 1932–present. It was the first manufacturer to introduce an all–stainless steel exterior; it also had distinctive curved rooflines and rounded glass block corners.

DeRaffle Manufacturing Company, New Rochelle, New York, 1933–present. Currently, it is the largest surviving diner manufacturer. In 1933, DeRaffele began to manufacture diners at the old Tierney plant. Earlier models were noted for their vertical fluting.

Fodero Dining Car Company, Bloomfield, New Jersey, 1933–81. It produced many exceptional diners throughout its long history and was noted for its famous winged clock.

Sterling Diners (J.B. Judkins Company), Merrimac, Massachusetts, 1936–42. It built carriages and motorcar bodies before turning to diners, creating one of the most distinctive models ever built: the Streamliner model, which mimicked the streamlined railroad cars of its day and featured either one or two rounded ends.

Valentine Manufacturing Company, Wichita, Kansas, 1938–74. It was the only significant diner manufacturer in its time that wasn't based in the Northeast. It built a small, boxy diner radically different than those produced by other manufacturers; the most popular model was the "Little Chef," an eight- or ten-stool one-man operation, with takeout service and finished in porcelain enamel or painted steel.

Mountain View Diners, Singac, New Jersey, 1939–57. Its trademark feature was a unique corner detail known as the "cowcatcher," marked by rounded corners that square off at the bottom. It went out of business shortly after attempting to go public.

Rochester Grills, Rochester, New York, 1940–?. It built diners in the same style as Bixler.

Orleans Manufacturing Company, Albion, New York, 1947–48. It built three diners.

Comac Inc., Irvington, New Jersey, 1947–51. Two Comac-built diners are still in existence today.

Master Diners, Pequannock, New Jersey, 1947–mid-1950. It was a small company that built stainless steel diners in two or three styles and various sizes.

Manno Dining Car Company, Fairfield, New Jersey, 1949–78. It was founded by Ralph Manno and Vincent Giannotti, both formerly with Kullman Diners. It was a diner renovation company turned manufacturer and built various styles of diners, including all-brick exterior "Colonial" diners. It crafted nearly all-glass façades and interesting stainless steel work.

Bramson Engineering Company, Oyster Bay, New York, mid-1950s. It was a hospital equipment manufacturer turned diner builder as a sideline.

Erfed Corporation, Rutherford, New Jersey, 1956–mid-1970. The company was started by Erwin Fedkenheuer Sr., former lead sheet metal man with Paramount Diners. It specialized in the repair, modernization and renovation of existing diners on location.

Campora Dining Car Company, Kearny, New Jersey, 1957. It was a short-lived manufacturing company started by Jerry Campora, a former shop supervisor at Kullman Diners; it may have only built one diner.

Swingle Diners, Middlesex, New Jersey, 1957–88. Previously, this company was involved in sales relationships with Fodero and Jerry O'Mahony before turning to diner manufacturing.

Diner-Mite Diners, Atlanta, Georgia, 1959–present. It builds modular food service units of varying shapes and sizes under names such as Module Mobile Inc. and Diner Group Limited.

Musi Dining Car Company, Carteret, New Jersey, 1966–present. Ralph Musi founded the company after departing from the Kullman Dining Car Company. It built new diners in the Colonial and Mediterranean styles.

Starlite Diners, Holly Hill, Florida, 1992–present. It offers a standard diner in mirror-finish stainless steel and has shipped diners all over the world. It builds Denny's Classic Diners for the Denny's restaurant chain.

Author's note: The history of lunch wagons and diners, as well as the manufacturers, is drawn from the groundbreaking research of Richard J.S. Gutman.

Counter Culture

I motorcycled down to New York City's Bleecker Street in 2003 for my first of several appearances at the legendary CBGB (Country, BlueGrass and Blues). The club, founded in 1973 by Hilly Kristal, was my first direct experience, both musically and personally, with the American punk counterculture. CBGB was the stage for the musical and social expression of such new-wave bands as the Ramones, the Misfits, Television, the Patti Smith Group, Mink DeVille, the Dead Boys, the Dictators, the Fleshtones, the Voidoids, the Cramps, the B-52s, Blondie, Joan Jett & the Blackhearts, the Shirts and Talking Heads. From the early 1980s until its later years, it would mainly become known for hardcore punk, with bands such as Agnostic Front, Murphy's Law, U.S. Chaos, Cro-Mags, Warzone, Gorilla Biscuits, Sick of It All and Youth of Today becoming synonymous with the club. While my own musical roots were more acoustic singer-songwriter—my influences being Simon & Garfunkel; Crosby, Stills, Nash and Young; Donovan; and the like—CBGB had become increasingly eclectic, embracing multiple musical styles and genres.

The CBGB punk counterculture was formed around a set of values and norms of behavior that deviated from that of mainstream society. In fact, it was often in direct opposition to the mores of the dominant culture. Sitting backstage at CBGB, waiting for my turn to perform, enabled me to feel and hear through the songs being played the ethos, aspirations and dreams of this rebellious albeit committed group of talented musicians. And like major countercultural movements such as Romanticism (1790–1840), Bohemianism (1850–1910), the Beat Generation (1944–1964) and the hippie counterculture (1964–1974), American punk's voice reached critical mass and triggered dramatic cultural and musical changes that continue today.

The diner "counter culture" is equally significant in its social pervasiveness, but experiencing a diner sitting at the counter is anything but contrary to mainstream society. It is, in fact, symbolic of it. As quintessentially American as domestic punk music, diners are the meeting place for the widest spectrum of nationalities and personalities in their owners, staff and patrons. Diners are emblematic of the pursuit and realization of the small business entrepreneurial dream and testament to the cultural diversity with which America is synonymous.

While punk rock held firm to its volitional alienation from the mainstream, popular TV eateries like Tom's Restaurant in New York City (*Seinfeld*), Arnold's (*Happy Days*) and Mel's Diner (*Alice*) popularized the diner as the cultural centerpiece of good times and home-grown happiness. Even the Downington Diner made famous in the classic 1958 horror film *The Blob* stood for safety and security. But just as punk music had its Vader-like musical and behavioral dark side, the "always open" diner serving late meals to third-shift factory workers and after-dark nightclub patrons became synonymous with loneliness, isolation and despair, popularized in Edward Hopper's iconic 1942 painting, *Nighthawks*. Hopper's greatest work, the painting powerfully plays dark against light with the neon, cherry wood counter, stools, bright metal tanks, jade green tiles, light walls and yellow kitchen door, creating a luminescent fish bowl of activity in stark contrast to the dark street outside, the dull gray diner foundation and roof and the muted green and red houses that appear lifeless. The characters, too, are a yin-yang of light and dark. A young waiter with blonde hair, coat and cap draws conversational looks from a young woman in a bright-red dress accompanied by a man in a dark suit, gray hat and blue shirt. This trio is juxtaposed across the diner counter from a solitary and sinister-looking male figure. Hopper's diner could be one of the many diners that were historically placed near factories that operated twenty-four hours a day, with third-shift workers and night owls providing a key part of the customer base.

As a rule, though, diners were symbols of American optimism—in particular, 1950s white American prosperity. Franchises like Denny's and Waffle House have attempted to copy the look of 1950s diners for nostalgic appeal in an attempt to replicate the classic diner interior. While both diners and fast-food chains provide customers with familiar and recognizable places to eat and meet, as well as put an emphasis on the consistent quality of the food made and served, classic diners retain their real relationship with the individual customer and the community, the guarded recipe for longevity and customer loyalty. The corporate food monoliths hedge their bets on the convenience and quick deliverability of assembly line food as the way to customers' return visits. The diner, on the other hand, creates the social experience of eating at home while away from home, with food as good as mom would make and friends always right nearby.

American comfort food is the calling card of classic diners, with hamburgers, French fries, club sandwiches and a milkshake synonymous with these classic eateries. Since most historic diners prepare food from a grill positioned directly behind the counter, almost all meals were cooked there, and no dividing lines existed between conversation and cuisine. Breakfast is the traditional flagship diner meal, with eggs, bacon, toast, pancakes and a fresh cup of strong coffee as uncomplicated as it needs to get. And just as the iconic classic diner has variations in design based on the creativity of its manufacturer, there are vicissitudinous variations in menu offerings depending on where one is regionally. A cross-country motorcycle ride has found me eating hot dogs in Ohio, fried pork tenderloin in Indiana, clams in Massachusetts, cheesesteaks in Pennsylvania, crab cakes in Maryland and cheesecake in New York. No matter where I am, I always get excited when the diner I'm in has that old-fashioned rotating cake and pie carousel, in front of which I sit mesmerized, forgetting the number of WW points in any selection in which I might be tempted to indulge.

Although we know that we can walk into an unfamiliar diner for the first time and feel totally comfortable sitting at a stool or even in a booth by ourselves when it's not busy, we don't go to the diner to be alone. We go there to belong, to feel welcomed. Fast-food chains play to the isolationism prevalent in our texting society such that we can drive up to the voice-without-a-face order machine, pay for our food at a window with someone we don't have to engage in conversation with, pick up our food at the next window in an inconspicuous paper bag that doesn't expose what we're eating to anyone else, drive but a few yards to an open parking space, roll up the windows, turn on the radio and never have to engage with another human being while we're eating. It's at a diner that we can be our authentic selves in the presence of others and feel as genuine as the meatloaf and potatoes. There's no dress code, no prescribed ritualistic "eating out" behavior and no cumbersome out-of-place feelings. A diner is as welcoming and comfortable as putting on your favorite pair of sneakers or sitting in your favorite chair in front of the television. You can order whatever you want off the experiential menu: solitude, camaraderie, conversation or silence. The diner is not a place you go to; rather, it's a place you've never left.

Unfortunately, classic diners, like many of the most cherished experiences we have grown up with, are disappearing from the American landscape. This book is more than just a book to me. It's more than a compilation of interesting diner facts and stories to serve as your guide when you visit these age-defiant symbols of the good times. This book is my attempt to preserve and hold on to what tomorrow might be gone from our list of favorite places. While diners represent the good times, many of them are running out of time in their failure to keep up with the current times despite herculean efforts. Bigger than diners themselves, the main streets on which they have resided and come to be associated with are themselves morphing into something unrecognizable. Sidewalks and the greetings exchanged by passersby are now text messages exchanged impersonally on the Internet highway. Conversations are keystrokes, and smiles are symbols inserted into texts. Shared emotions arrive in e-mails as additional exclamation points, and the contagion of a deep, genuine laugh is lost in the "LOL." Getting to know someone is now "gting 2 no u," and the joy of walking in on your own surprise party is minimized to "OMG!" on one's mobile device.

Individuality is a value I hold sacred. I feel it when I motorcycle. I encourage it in my children on their journeys toward real self-actualization. It is the characteristic I look to draw out of the guests I interview on my radio show. It is my motivation when I perform. It is the trait I feel so consistently from diner owners I talk with who have immigrated to this country, left all things familiar behind and braved the unknowns of small business entrepreneurship with nothing more than an ethic of hard work, some savings and a belief in how others should be treated. At this moment in our cultural history, when fast-food franchises double-speak to having it your way so long as it's on the drive-up menu, cookie-cutter cultural composting is antithetical to the individuality of the American spirit. The classic diner is one of the last truly interactive conduits we have to connect the past with the present and ensure our future values.

Fairfield County

Fairfield County occupies 836.96 square miles of southwestern Connecticut and is the most densely populated county in the Nutmeg State, boasting almost 1,500 people per square mile. It also contains four of the largest cities in the state: Bridgeport, Stamford, Norwalk and Danbury. Fairfield County is one of the wealthiest counties in the United States in per capita income, garnering the title of "the Gold Coast" in recognition of its affluence.

There are many transportation arteries pumping Fairfield County's heart, including the parallel-running Interstate 95 and scenic Merritt Parkway. The Merritt Parkway is one of my favorite rides because it is a truck-free scenic highway and does not overwhelm one with the commercial traffic so evident on I-95. In addition to Fairfield County also being fed by Interstate 84, U.S. Route 7, Connecticut Route 8 and Connecticut Route 25, the oldest east–west route in the country, U.S. 1 (aka the Boston Post Road), traverses the shoreline cities and towns, giving the traveler and diner aficionado a more local flavor en route to some of Connecticut's most wonderful classic diners, including Curley's Diner in Stamford, a renovated but mint 1949 Mountain View; the 1957 DeRaffele-built, space age–styled Parkway Diner in Stamford; the painstakingly restored Post Road Diner in Norwalk manufactured by Paramount in 1947; Norwalk's Family Diner, a 1955 Mountain View production that is almost wholly original; Bridgeport landmark White's Diner built in 1957 by DeRaffele; and its down-the-street neighbor, the Hi Way Diner, manufactured by Musi in about 1967.

To engage in conversations with the owners of classic diners in Connecticut brings one deep into the history of the Greeks who arrived in large numbers after 1945 as they fled the economic devastation caused by World War II and the Greek Civil War. Almost 250,000 immigrants from Greece came to the United States. During the decades of the '50s, '60s and '70s, more than six hundred diners were started by Greek immigrants in the New York area alone, and nowhere are their contributions more readily apparent than in Fairfield County, Connecticut. The trend of Greek immigrants starting as dishwashers and then becoming busboys, short-order cooks and, ultimately, owners is a familiar theme that sews the heritage of the diners together, as are the rock-solid work ethic and commitment to the business and its customers. While the combined impact of the fast-food culture, the profit-driven priorities of financial institutions, the demolishing of these historic eateries under the guise of progress and the next generation of family members taking their parents' realized dream of a college education for them and moving out of the family-run diner business to pursue other careers has put the future of many diners in jeopardy, these wonderful community-based eateries are available to us today. For the fair price of a wonderfully prepared meal served by friendly waitstaff in a social setting, we can take a journey back in time and embrace the values and experiences that are the hallmarks of classic diners.

CURLEY'S DINER
62 PARK PLACE, STAMFORD
1949 MOUNTAIN VIEW

Almost completely renovated and bearing little resemblance to the original diner owned and managed by Herluf "Curley" Svenningsen, Curley's Diner retains its humble place as a "local diner" while being a modern-day David and Goliath story of sister-owners Maria Aposporos and Eleni Bergetis taking on city hall to prevent Curley's from being bulldozed into urban obscurity.

Maria began working as a waitress in the diner in 1976 when her husband's death made generating additional income a necessity. "You learn to do whatever it takes," she shared with me. "You don't lose your pride when you do tough, physical work. You find it under the toughest circumstances." It took only a year for Maria's entrepreneurial spirit to show itself when she bought the diner in 1977. Her penchant for working hard when she punched the clock as a waitress is even more evident in her now as the owner of what continues to be a diner open 24/7. "I used to work all day and all night with no days off. If you have a diner, you have to be here and be involved with everything going on every day. The diner is your life. That's part of the reason that my customers have become family."

Today, Curley's Diner serves good food at affordable prices around the clock as a family operation. "I work mornings. My younger sister, Eleni, and her daughter work afternoons, and my son works nights. We make sure that one of us is always here to take care of our customers personally. Being a diner owner is really something you can't delegate. So much of the success of a diner depends on the relationships we build. People expect that when they come here, the food will be good. But they also expect to feel welcomed and at home. You can't teach someone how to create those kinds of bonds."

One cannot talk with Maria Aposporos and be anything but impressed with her Greek immigrant success story of rolling up her sleeves, waiting on customers, saving her money and then buying the very diner where she worked. She speaks to the core of every successful entrepreneur who knows that to make it you pay the price of 'round-the-clock commitment and hard work. It also emanates from the passion of doing what you are meant to do and going after the singular purpose in life with which you identify your innermost being. It's a recurring theme in classic diners and the hardworking people who own and operate them.

The story of Maria's success running Curley's Diner since 1977 and her hard work ethic born and honed out of her compassion for giving her customers the best home-cooked food whenever they want it is but one part of a greater success story. After Curley's three decades of uninterrupted service to its customers, the City of Stamford attempted to take Curley's Diner from Maria on the grounds of eminent domain to make way for an apartment building. The city went so far as to exert additional pressure on Maria to give up the property by erecting a chain link fence on the property it owned adjacent to the diner, in effect making it impossible for customers to use the parking lot. Unable to easily access the diner, garbage trucks had difficulty removing the trash, for which the City of Stamford quickly issued health code violations.

However, Maria was unaware of the adage, "You can't fight city hall." She had been raised in a Spartan family of several generations of male members who were high-ranking officers in the Greek military. "We were taught as children," Maria proudly declared, pushing her finger into the counter tabletop to drive her point home, "never to take anything from anybody and to stand up for ourselves." And that's exactly what she did. She fought back, and after spending more than $250,000 in legal fees, she won a Connecticut Supreme Court case that enabled her to keep Curley's Diner. She was never offered the millions of dollars that are alleged to have been the City of Stamford's "official" conciliatory offer. The amount was actually $233,000, a far cry from what would have been the city's $4.6 million turnaround selling price to the developer!

Maria and her family continue to offer a full array of American and Greek food from a menu whose cover proudly declares, "God Bless America." She doesn't gloat over her court decision or stand on a soapbox all day boasting of her accomplishments. On the contrary, Maria sits in her booth near the door where she commands all the activity taking place at Curley's Diner and solemnly reflects on its fate: "Stamford is new now, different. My own customers die, and the younger generation has moved. No one can afford to stay here. As long as my sister, Eleni, and I survive, Curley's will survive. After that, I don't know. The new generation doesn't have the same connection to diners that we have."

Curley's Diner serves basic American diner fare, with breakfast a specialty. In fact, the specials include eggs Benedict as the lead-off item. From there, bacon, ham or sausage can accompany two eggs any style, griddlecakes, French toast, golden brown waffles, a vegetarian omelette, the Lumberjack (which pairs three pancakes with two eggs), eggs and a hamburger (for those undecided between breakfast and lunch), corned beef hash and eggs, the Trucker's Special (served with three eggs any style, potatoes, toast, bacon, ham and sausage) and a gyro (for the Greek American palate). The griddlecakes come with a range of accompaniments, including blueberries, strawberries, bananas or chocolate chips. For omelette lovers, there are thirteen to choose from, of which the corned beef or pastrami omelettes are the ones that never fail to test my decision-making ability. There are pastries aplenty to choose from: corn muffins, blueberry muffins, bran muffins, English muffins, pound cake, cinnamon toast or the simple diner staple, a buttered roll.

You don't have to limit yourself to breakfast items at Curley's Diner, not by a long shot. There are some wonderfully delicious surprises on the menu, like the Ranger, a specially seasoned New York strip steak sandwich served with an egg, French fries and a pickle, and the filet mignon covered with bordelaise sauce, tips of sparrowgrass and baby corn that in itself warrants a visit to Curley's just to say you had it. Greek

Left: Maria Aposporos, owner of Curley's Diner.

Below: An early photo of Curley's Diner in downtown Stamford.

Curley's Diner today.

specialties like the chicken souvlaki platter and the gyro platter underscore the international flavor that awaits you. Or you can visit the Italian section of the menu and select from spaghetti and meatballs or chicken parmigiana. Think as big as you want to when it comes to dinner specials, served with soup or salad, potato or rice and vegetables. There's sirloin steak with mushrooms and onion rings, broiled pork chops, broiled liver and onions, prime rib with mushroom caps and onion rings, charbroiled rib eye steak, grilled chicken and broiled leg of lamb.

From the fountain at Curley's Diner, you can treat yourself to an old-fashioned egg cream, stand your straw up in a thick milkshake or go daydreaming about the past with your hand wrapped around an ice cream soda topped with whipped cream. Pull the belt out a notch and have at least a forkful of the cream cheese cake or strawberry shortcake. They're downright decadent.

Whatever food you select, savor it as part of the Curley's Diner experience. A classic diner is no place to visit when you're in a rush. The experience is all about stopping time for a few moments to let yourself be transported back to when life was simpler and values were evident and unchanging. A strong cup of fresh coffee is the elixir of life. As David Letterman said, "If it wasn't for the coffee, I'd have no identifiable personality whatsoever."

PARKWAY DINER
1066 HIGH RIDGE ROAD, STAMFORD
1957 DeRAFFELE

Taking its name from the scenic Merritt Parkway, which is an easy-on, easy-off route to the Parkway Diner, the Jetsonsian exterior captures the space-age optimism prevalent in the designs of its builder, DeRaffele. You cannot help but feel like you're stepping into a culinary Disneyland Space Mountain when you enter this fabulous structure with its winged entranceway and abundance of gleaming rocket ship–like stainless steel.

The interior of the Parkway Diner is not too reflective of its predecessor, the Country Diner, but the menu and friendliness of the staff make up for what was the inside of the Parkway's predecessor. The meatloaf dinner I sampled was wonderful enough to take on the competition of what my mother would make for Sunday evening supper, and the chicken parmigiana would satiate the most selective Italian. There's nothing that beats breakfast at a diner, and the pancakes at the Parkway Diner are superior to those made and served in area pancake specialty restaurants. David's Harvest multigrain nut pancakes are complemented by their touted female counterpart, Charlotte's Pancakes, which are more like crepes and are served with fresh fruit. Both are billed as "Champion Buttermilk Pancakes" at the Parkway Diner, and for me, there has never been a clear winner; both are phenomenal! In addition to those top-billing griddlecakes, there are also blueberry, chocolate, banana and silver dollar pancakes served in short or tall stacks. Add some ham, bacon or sausage, and it's a feast fit for a king. If you prefer waffles, the selection is equally impressive: Belgian, blueberry, chocolate chip, banana and banana brown sugar. You can even have a homemade doughnut with your coffee. The portions of the food served are testament to the abundant supply of take-home containers readily available. It's simply too much food for one sitting (excluding mine).

Lunch offerings are equally delicious, with bountiful portion sizes. There are cold sandwiches, including fresh roast beef, turkey, ham and cheese, the classic BLT, egg salad, tuna salad and chicken salad. The hot sandwiches, all served with French fries, lead off with Jennifer's Creation of smoked turkey, apples and brie cheese on multigrain bread with salad. There's also a corned beef Reuben, California grilled chicken, a barbecue chicken supermelt, chicken or pork souvlaki, beef gyro, traditional tuna melt, BBQ shredded pork and a hot open-face turkey or roast beef. Wedges include a Philly cheese steak, chicken parmigiana, eggplant parmigiana, meatball parmigiana, veal parmigiana and one of my favorites at the Parkway Diner, Joanie & Jan's boneless BBQ pork. Wraps include roast beef, grilled chicken, tuna, Mexican, crunchy and veggie, and for salad lovers, there is an equally wide variety. And like any classic diner, there are beef, turkey and veggie burgers aplenty.

With fewer diners open beyond breakfast and lunch, eating dinner at the Parkway Diner is a special treat. There's a complete beer and wine list to sip from while selecting appetizers from a list that includes nachos, Parkway's Famous Chili, chicken quesadilla, firecracker chicken wings, fried mozzarella sticks, cheese fries, chili cheese French fries, onion rings and sweet potato French fries. But those are just the invitation to the dinner, the selections of which are impressive: pot roast, New York strip, broiled pork chops, chopped steak, rib eye, stuffed peppers or stuffed cabbage, Texas baby back ribs, chicken marsala, chicken Francaise, lemon chicken, grilled chicken, grilled salmon, crab cakes, London-style fish and chips and blackened swordfish. For the Italian food lover, there's shrimp and scallops Alfredo, pasta primavera, bowtie chicken, penne alla vodka, fettuccine Alfredo, chicken scarpariello, linguine fra diavolo, Old World–style eggplant parmigiana, chicken parmigiana and veal parmigiana. And the pièce de résistance is a slice of New York–style cheesecake as good as you'd get in any of the five boroughs, as well as chocolate mousse cake.

The secret sauce of great food combined with friendly service is no accident at the Parkway Diner. The Oz-like wizard behind the curtain controlling all facets of the experience is Lushe Gjuraj, who came into serendipitous ownership following several minimum wage, part-time jobs working at the Stamford-based Lakeside Diner peeling potatoes, washing dishes and waiting on tables for almost a decade. When she lost her full-time computer-related job and faced the need to take care of a growing family, the segue from part-time diner work to diner ownership tapped into her own entrepreneurial DNA. Unlike many people who, when they lose a job, jump at the most readily available work to bring income into the household, she saw her adversity as an opportunity to fulfill her own dream of working for herself. With the generous support of family members, an accommodating banker and dipping into her savings, Lushe went full speed into creating the ideal diner experience. "I love cooking and working with people. I love making people happy and making their day," she proudly declared. Reflecting back on the scariness of losing her computer career but seeing the alternative opportunity it presented, she learnedly commented, "When

Parkway Diner interior.

you have all your eggs in one basket and your dreams go away, you say to yourself, 'What am I going to do now?' Fortunately, I found the answer in my own heart. I am so blessed because I found out that I am exactly where I am supposed to be. I can live with risk, but I can't live with regret."

A Yugoslavian immigrant, Lushe Gjuraj came to the United States at the age of seventeen. Never forgetting her roots and her extended family abroad, she used her savings to help twenty-four relatives escape war-torn Kosovo and find freedom and opportunity in Stamford. Patrons of the Parkway Diner not only find diversity in the menu itself, but on one occasion, I was also greeted by a Brazilian hostess, served by a Bulgarian waitress and paid my check to a German cashier. The Parkway Diner is not only a haven for hungry travelers but also symbolizes in its embrace of all who enter how important freedom is and how so many immigrants simply crave the chance to contribute to society and make a home for themselves and their families. When Lushe proudly declares the United States to be "the best country in the world," you know that what you experience at the Parkway Diner will be a culinary as well as cultural blue plate special.

POST ROAD DINER
312 CONNECTICUT AVENUE, NORWALK
1947 PARAMOUNT

Teddy Giapoutzis was working for a food service company and servicing the Post Road Diner when a client, John Papadatos, offered to sell him the diner. While the notion of owning and managing a twenty-four-hour restaurant did not initially appeal to him, the idea of owning the Post Road Diner did, and so Teddy, his wife, Olga, his two sisters and his brother-in-law combined resources and scheduled their time around making the 24/7 operation work. But it would take more than rotating shifts to create the diner experience that Teddy envisioned and ultimately realized.

When Teddy purchased the Post Road Diner in 1995, it was in need of a major overhaul. The maintenance and cleaning of the interior had lapsed, and the exterior was hidden behind brick. With the help and advice of diner manufacturer Phil DeRaffele himself (whom Teddy affectionately refers to as the "godfather of diners"), Teddy completely renovated the interior, added a new kitchen, converted the basement crawlspace into a full storage area the size of the diner perimeter itself, redesigned the entire interior and upgraded the exterior of the diner so that it sparkled inside and out.

The menu was transformed into a home cooking lover's nirvana, with enough variety of omelettes to appeal to every taste. There are seven "creative" omelettes, including the veggie, lite, farmer's, Post Road Diner burrito, Tuscan, low carb and California. Among my personal favorites are the Post Road Breakfast Burrito, including sausage, onions, peppers, eggs and pepper jack cheese served in a flour tortilla with salsa and sour cream, and the Tuscan Omelette, with roasted peppers, portobello, mozzarella and pesto. There are also eleven additional omelettes, each one worthy of trying.

The Post Road Diner also offers a wide selection of pancakes, from the basic buttermilk griddlecakes to blueberry; blueberry and ricotta; banana and walnuts; chocolate chips; and buckwheat (my favorite). There are Belgian waffles; waffles and fruit; the Waffles Supreme, with a scoop of ice cream and strawberries or peaches and cream; the breakfast waffle, with Canadian bacon, scrambled eggs and melted cheese; the Jungle Waffle, with banana and nut topping, chocolate chips and caramel syrup; the Blueberry Hill Waffle; the Chip Chip Hurray Waffle, made with blueberries and whipped cream; and the bacon waffle with scrambled eggs and cheese.

Teddy Giapoutzis, owner of the Post Road Diner.

Interior of the Post Road Diner.

Post Road Diner sign.

As with any classic diner, if it's not on the menu, they'll make it special for you. Post Road Diner French toast is also a multi-selection staple, from the old-fashioned kind to homemade varieties, French toast dipped in coconut, homemade cinnamon raisin or whole wheat. And any order can be accompanied by home fries, corned beef hash, bacon, sausage, ham, turkey sausage, turkey bacon, Canadian bacon or a side of toast. There's always plenty of chilled fresh fruit, grits and oatmeal on hand, as well as a full assortment of muffins and croissants.

While breakfasts are the Post Road Diner's opening act, there is an equally daunting menu of lunch selections, including sixteen types of salads, twelve pizzas with a variety of toppings, a calzone with ricotta and mozzarella, seventeen deli sandwiches, ten club sandwiches, eleven burgers and twenty kinds of grinders. But wait, there's more. The Post Road Diner's "fancy sandwiches," of which there are fourteen, include four types of wraps, a Cuban sandwich, a French dip sandwich, a grilled vegetable panini, Texas-style BBQ meatloaf, pesto grilled chicken, Cajun chicken and prime rib.

As you turn the pages of the Post Road Diner menu, breakfast and lunch items are but a gateway to a lineup of dinners that leave one breathless, especially at the end of the meal. There are twenty appetizers, with several standouts, such as the homemade spinach pie, dolmades, quesadillas, calamari, grilled zucchini, Buffalo fingers and Teddy's Casserole, made up of waffle fries topped with chili, bacon bits and mozzarella. Specialty dinners play to Teddy's Greek influences, with pork souvlaki, chicken souvlaki, gyros and Mamma's Moussaka. There's also eggplant parmigiana, chicken breast parmigiana and chicken Francaise. Of the fifteen pasta items, the standouts are the whole wheat ziti, Gemelli chicken and all of the pennes. Among the classic diner offerings are baked meatloaf, baked stuffed peppers, roast turkey, hot open-face roast beef, liver, bacon and onions and chicken breast cordon bleu. Shrimp scampi, fresh salmon (awesome!) and clam strips highlight the nine available seafood dinners, and for steak and chop lovers, there are New York sirloin, T-bone, flank and Mediterranean flank cuts, all grilled to perfection.

You can wash down your meal with a "real deal" malt like the Oreo shake, banana shake, hot fudge shake or chocolate peanut butter shake, and no Post Road Diner meal is complete until it's topped off with homemade desserts created by Olga right in her on-site bakery.

The large stand-alone neon street sign that invites hungry travelers in off Connecticut Avenue is a thing of beauty, but it is not the only surprise that awaits patrons before they enter the diner. Teddy also purchased the building adjacent to the Post Road Diner that formerly housed Phil's Machine Shop and bookends the diner parking lot. Sitting in one of his own booths one day, Teddy looked out and contemplated the huge wall facing the diner. He decided to integrate it into the retro feel that he had painstakingly created for the Post Road Diner. Remembering the Starlite Drive-In Theater that once occupied the land behind the diner from 1950 to 1983, he hired the late Czechoslovakian artist and Stamford resident Zora to paint a grand mural depicting the Starlite Drive-In, with a scene from the classic 1942 film *Casablanca* starring Humphrey Bogart and Ingrid Bergman. After viewing the mural, one cannot help but paraphrase Captain Louis Renault's (Claude Rains) famous line: "Everybody comes to the Post Road Diner."

Reflecting on his original reason for almost not purchasing the Post Road Diner (the challenges of running a 24/7 diner), Teddy remarked:

The economy has hurt us a lot. But what has hurt us the most is that so many area businesses used to be open twenty-four hours when we purchased

Post Road Diner exterior.

Post Road Diner mural by Zora.

the diner. Local retailers like Dunkin' Donuts, Pathmark Supermarkets and the gas stations used to depend on the third-shift workers to purchase from them as well. Three major factories, including Valeries Trucking, ran three shifts. We had a full staff working our own third shift just to accommodate all the patrons who wanted a good meal. Now there are no third-shift workers, and the chain gas stations operate twenty-four hours, serving sandwiches and coffee as well as fuel.

The number of fast-food chains that have popped up on Connecticut Avenue has further affected the business the Post Road Diner used to serve. "Places like McDonald's can afford to be open twenty-four hours. They only need two employees to handle the drive-in customers, and serving food from a drive-up window is safer. You never have to open the front door. People don't want to get out of their cars anymore. They don't take the time today to sit and eat anymore. It's a different world." Teddy knows that it takes more than convenience to create a true classic diner experience. "The difference between a diner and a chain is that people go to diners for the personality, as well as the home cooking. People continue to frequent diners because of the special attention they get there. A lot of people want that extra attention. It's all about making people welcome at the Post Road Diner. You greet them like an old friend who comes into your home."

FAMILY DINER
71 MAIN STREET, NORWALK
1955 MOUNTAIN VIEW #480

Family Diner owner Phil Kydes loves old things. Whether it's reminiscing about his 1959 Cadillac, displaying decades-old black-and-white photos or sharing with pride his original ownership papers for the diner, Phil is all about nostalgia and preserving memories of earlier times. "I wanted to create a diner experience that people would remember as I did. When I came home from college for family visits, my first stop was always the Family Diner. Only after visiting the diner did I then go to my house. I promised myself that one day it would be mine." And Phil made good on that promise. "I never thought of the Family Diner as a business. Rather, I had always thought of the diner as a way for people to feel the way I do about antiquity and to re-experience the past as we actually lived it. Countless memories come to mind when I think back about what it felt like for me to be young and visit the Family Diner. So many people over the years have come through here and appreciated the diner for different reasons. It meant different, special things for each person."

Classic diners are synonymous with the sense of "family" and feeling "at home," whether you're with a group or dining alone. You can't build those intangible qualities into a modern diner by simply printing on the menu that a restaurant is a "family" diner. You can't purchase '50s tchotchkes on eBay and fill the walls with them to create a sense of legacy. These feelings of "belongingness" are part of the DNA of classic diners and grow over time through actual experiences. "Joel Bloom and his brother, Willy Bloom, owned the Family Diner before me," recalled Phil Kydes. "Though he never deliberately brought attention to them, the tattooed memories of Auschwitz were permanently inked into his arms. The diner was his dream for a new beginning. Joel raised his family in the diner, where they did their homework and played. My own daughters grew up in the Family Diner after I bought it and still work here when I need them. It's called the Family Diner for a reason. For our extended family of patrons, it's also their home—a place where they belong and are appreciated."

The Family Diner boasts a classic exterior that is an irresistible wave to come in, much like memories of one's mother holding the front door open with a smile that said "welcome home" when you grew up and returned for a visit. And the same goes for the interior. The thirteen booths and thirteen stools are original, save the refurbished coverings. The terrazzo floors joining the sections of the L-shaped dining area are original as well. "My goal when I purchased the Family Diner was to maintain the look and feel of it—what I consider its integrity. People's personalities are what they are and are different from person to person. And even though a person can behave differently at different times, genuine personality is what it is. The same goes for a diner's personality. The more you are true to who or what you really are, the more genuine will be others' experiences of you."

Phil Kydes is experiencing the same economic strain that other classic diner owners are feeling, and he is responding to the pressures much the way any concerned head of a family would. "The economy has taken its toll and challenges us to literally keep our doors open. I have struggled to keep the Family Diner open and am committed to doing just that because of my workers. Every decision I make is with regards to how it will affect them. They depend on me. Their families depend on me to be successful. My staff works here to pay their mortgages and to send their children to school. I need to make sure they are okay. We are family. I am responsible to them."

At the Family Diner, don't expect a modern version of a diner with the menu displayed on big-screen TV monitors in each corner of the ceiling and a forty-page menu that requires a day of preparation to get through it. This diner is the real deal—a classic that has stood the test of time and evokes the value of basic diner fare served by waitstaff who are more like your aunts and uncles than paid employees. There's nothing fancy or frilly about the Family Diner, and this gives it the charm it evokes. What you will experience is sitting among a lot of locals and sharing an impromptu conversation or passing the local newspaper with ad-libbed commentary about how the local high school sports team fared at the game the night before or different opinions on what the town representatives voted on.

Breakfast is the stage-setter at the Family Diner. You can have eggs served any way you like, fried up or down or poached, with a bagel, toast, a roll or muffins and home fries, as well as a side of Canadian bacon, sausage or hash. There are also fried eggs and western sandwiches, which are the frequent early morning to-go requests. French toast and pancakes, including blueberry and chocolate chip, are always options, as are oatmeal and cereal. There are twenty sandwiches to choose from for lunch, as well as burgers with cheese, bacon, mushroom, pizza sauce and/or chili. There are ample triple-decker sandwiches served with French fries, bacon, lettuce, tomato and a pickle. And you can always ask for a side order of French fries with gravy, chili or melted cheese, onion rings, coleslaw and more. For those watching their calories, there are several cold salad and diet salad platters to choose from. Standard diner fare entrées served with potatoes and vegetables include meatloaf, roast beef, roast turkey, grilled chicken breast, chopped steak, franks with baked beans, southern fried chicken, ham steak, beef liver, breaded veal platter and breaded veal parmigiana. Seafood catches include shrimp, sole, clams and scallops.

The "specials" section of the Family Diner menu is where I usually focus my attention. It boasts a New York strip open steak sandwich, pastrami with melted cheese, a pastrami or corned beef grilled Reuben, tuna melt on whole wheat bread, Monte Carlo grilled ham, shrimp in the basket and the standard but wonderfully delicious patty melt. Always check the day's specials menu. I stumbled across a beef stew quite by accident that was amazing.

Owner Phil Kydes of Family Diner and his daughter, Kiki.

Family Diner exterior.

Family Diner interior.

Bring your appetite to the Family Diner, where you will find not only a place at the counter to enjoy your meal and some friendly conversation but also an environment where all dreams are welcome and all of life's challenges given a break. Experience Phil Kydes's dream come true of re-creating the classic diner experience.

WHITE'S DINER
280 BOSTON AVENUE/ROUTE 1, BRIDGEPORT
1957 DeRAFFELE

White's Diner is a historical and cultural landmark in Bridgeport. Greg and Linda Cerminara are the fourth owners in a lineage started by Jack and Mabel White. Greg and his two brothers purchased the diner from their father, Ralph, and their uncle, Angelo Caruso, and it's been in the Cerminara family since 1977, with Greg now being the only one of the brothers in ownership. Other than the names on the title, little has changed physically to White's Diner since the days when Jack and Mabel first welcomed patrons inside. Except for the bathrooms, which were added by Greg after the original structure was built, the exterior is basically intact. On the inside, the stools and booths are re-covered but original, as is the counter. Nostalgic photos from the early days of Bridgeport are displayed proudly on the counter and throughout the diner, along with a photo of Al Pacino, who starred in the movie *Righteous Kill*, which was filmed at White's Diner.

Greg Cerminara came to the United States from Italy in 1957 and attended Harding High School. Upon graduation, he enlisted in the U.S. Air Force, with tours of duty in Japan, Korea and Vietnam. When he talks about his return to Bridgeport after Vietnam, you can feel the pain in Greg's voice over the cold reception that he and his comrades received. "We were the victims of a very unpopular war. Nobody thanked us for being there because they didn't support the Vietnam War like people did World Wars I and II. All we wanted to do was serve our country, and we felt condemned for it." As an ongoing attempt at recompense, Greg offered men and women in the armed services free breakfasts on Memorial Day in 2010. He did it again on Independence Day and now does it routinely for any active-duty military personnel from any branch of the service. "I put food on the table for these soldiers," Greg proudly declared, "but they put their lives on the line for us so we can enjoy all of the freedoms we have today. I don't ever want to forget to appreciate their sacrifices."

Greg's generosity goes beyond the military patrons he honors to all of his White's Diner customers, which is why this special eatery occupies such an important place in local Bridgeport culture.

I came from Italy with nothing but my own determination and worked hard to the point where I can sincerely say that I am proud of and thankful for what White's Diner stands for. I always have soup on the stove and give it away before my last customers leave as a way of saying "thank you" and "take care of yourself." At Thanksgiving, I host a free dinner for the people from a nearby shelter. We are part of the community, so we must be community-minded and take responsibility for our fellow citizens.

Greg's generosity comes from a big heart and not deep pockets. He knows what it's like to struggle and live on the edge, trying to sustain White's Diner in a challenging economic landscape. In fact, the diner almost didn't make it a few years ago when state road construction on Boston Avenue cut his business by more than half and customers found it difficult to enter the parking lot. To make matters worse, his taxes doubled at the same time. "I never got bitter and always found something to thank God for," he said, a comment that characterizes the person Greg is. "People come to White's Diner because it's family. For many, it is their home. There's nothing fancy inside, no disco lights, no loud music. The atmosphere is all about making contact with the customers. They become friends. If I don't see the regulars for a week, I wonder about them and worry about them. I call them up and ask if everything's all right. When they're sick, I bring them food. It's all about family."

The assortment of specialty omelettes is what Greg is most proud of. The list includes the steak omelette, Greg's Own Italian Omelette, a farmer's omelette, a veggie omelette, the Good Start Omelette, a three-cheese omelette, a spicy chili cheddar cheese omelette and others for a total of thirteen. And you can even create your own omelette from a lengthy list of fresh ingredients. "We make all kinds of omelettes because breakfast is our specialty and lunch is just an extension of breakfast." You can also have eggs any style, poached eggs and real egg whites, with side orders of bacon, ham, sausage, pastrami, grits and more, as well as bagels, assorted muffins and rolls if you don't want toast. You can have a short or tall stack of traditional griddlecakes or order from the specialty pancake menu of pecan, strawberry, blueberry, banana or chocolate chip delights.

Although Greg will tell you that breakfast is the perpetual meal at White's Diner, he humbly understates the lunch menu, which is equally varied and fresh. There are a whopping thirty-three sandwiches, including all variations of hamburgers and grilled cheeses, as well as the Reuben, Philly steak with cheese and chicken cutlet parmigiana. When the sun starts to set, the dinner items shine. The Italian specialties are a trademark of White's Diner, including the cavatelli with chicken and broccoli, the parmigiana with ziti and the ziti and sausage. Among the classic diner fare offerings are the baked meatloaf, breaded chicken cutlet, ham steak with pineapple ring, beef liver with onions and bacon, the terrific pot roast, roast sirloin of beef and roast turkey with gravy. No matter what you order, you are ensured a great meal in quantities that will challenge you.

Bridgeport is the most populous city in Connecticut, with a 2010 census calculation of 144,229 residents, and it is the fifth-largest city in New England (behind Boston, Worcester, Providence and Springfield).

Owner Greg Cerminara of White's Diner.

White's Diner interior.

White's Diner exterior.

Bridgeport is the center of the forty-eighth-largest urban area in the United States, just behind Hartford. While once a thriving trade, shipbuilding and whaling center, the village rapidly industrialized in the mid-nineteenth century, attracting immigrants to the growing number of factory jobs. The prosperity remained strong past World War II until industrial restructuring and suburbanization caused the loss of many jobs and affluent residents, leaving Bridgeport with extensive poverty. The conversion of office buildings to residential complexes and other redevelopment projects are attracting new residents to Bridgeport, but the economic strain continues and White's Diner feels the impact. But Gerg Cerminara continues to maintain White's Diner as a community eatery and meeting place, making sure that his family of longtime patrons continues to feel at home. Greg's temperament and White's Diner itself are synonymous with the words of circus promoter and former mayor P.T. Barnum, a famous resident of the city who built three houses there and housed his circus in town during winters: "The noblest art is that of making others happy."

HI WAY DINER
2025 BOSTON AVENUE/ROUTE 1, BRIDGEPORT
CIRCA 1967 MUSI

The Hi Way Diner architecturally epitomizes the Colonial and Mediterranean styles created by Ralph Musi, owner of the Carteret, New Jersey–based Musi Dining Car Company, in homage to his former employer, the Kullman Dining Car Company. Traveling along Boston Avenue (aka Route 1) in Bridgeport en route to Stratford, one cannot help but smile at the optimistic appearance of this entrenched roadside icon. Although the interior has changed considerably from its original appearance, the quality of the food and the friendliness with which it's served have been consistent.

The loyal patrons of the Hi Way Diner are the extended family of the owners—George, Gina, Anna and Maria Lycoudes—and this accounts for the immediate sense of kinship you feel sitting among the customers and overhearing the conversations. It's like taking a seat at a big dining room table with all the relatives present. And like any head of household hosting a family gathering, George, with his trademark towel draped over his shoulder, checks in on everyone to make sure that the food is to their liking and inquires about how they're doing in general. "The keys to the success we've had here at the Hi Way Diner are pretty basic," shared George. "We prepare good food from good ingredients, keep the place clean, maintain fair prices and

Hi Way Diner outside.

Hi Way Diner owner George Lycoudes.

always, always pay attention to the customer." It's this Hi Way Diner recipe for success that keeps loyal customers coming back. "We're not located near any major highway like Interstate 95 or the Merritt Parkway. But we are on U.S. 1, which used to be the main road before 95 was constructed."

And if the nostalgic appearance of the Hi Way isn't enough to make you turn off Route 1 into the parking lot, the aroma of home cooking making its way from the kitchen to the road surely will. The crispy fried chicken is prepared from a long-standing family recipe that accounts for it being so finger-licking good. The menu is basic diner fare, but you can't take for granted any single item tasting like what you've had somewhere else. For example, the mashed potatoes are homemade, with a touch of unique seasoning that takes it to an entirely new level. And the meatloaf and stuffed peppers are culinary delights. There are plenty of seats (sixteen stools, sixteen booths and eight tables) at the diner to accommodate the large crowds that often come in.

New Haven County

New Haven County is located in the south-central part of the state of Connecticut. The 2010 census tallied the county population at close to 1 million (862,477 to be exact), making it the third-most populated county in Connecticut. Two of the state's largest cities, New Haven (second) and Waterbury (fifth), are contained within its borders. New Haven County serves as a center of advanced learning within the state, with several noted educational institutions such as Albertus Magnus College, Gateway Community College, Naugatuck Valley Community College, Paier College of Art, Post University, Quinnipiac University, Southern Connecticut State University, the University of New Haven and Yale University. What better county than New Haven, with its aggregate and perpetually hungry student body, to have a diner?

U.S. Route 1 in New Haven County is a yellow brick road when it comes to discovering classic diners. Although it has been replaced by Interstate 95 as a through route, Route 1 travels parallel to it along an east–west heading (although most signs refer to its actual north–south orientation). The road runs shadow to Long Island Sound as a local Connecticut business route and an alternate to heavy commuter congestion on I-95 during rush hours. Route 1 and connected arteries to it are dotted with classic diners welcoming travelers in for a home-cooked meal and friendly conversation as they did before Interstate 95 diverted the bulk of traffic away from them. Among the diner treasures you'll find in New Haven County are the endearing Cassidy's Diner in Meriden from the 1949 Silk City production line, the rare

1954 Kullman "dinette" model personified by Tony's Diner in Seymour, the gleaming stainless steel and neon of Georgie's Diner in West Haven and Waterbury's Tower Grill. It's a lost pleasure, slowing life down and cruising along Route 1 to take in the shops and scenery, and it is well worth the detour from the rush-hour rituals and fast-food frenzies to savor the diner experience of yesterday.

CASSIDY'S DINER
82 WEST MAIN STREET, MERIDEN
1949 SILK CITY #49212

Cassidy's Diner (aka Cassidies Diner) owner Jay Eagle Delaney has a simple philosophy by which he's operated his establishment for more than a decade: "The first time you come in here you're a customer; the second time you're a friend; and the third time you're family." But the stainless steel classic is currently more of an iron lung attempting to stave off the last breath of its economic life. Jay is desperately doing what he can in order to sustain Cassidy's Diner as a longtime home to its loyal patrons, but it is an uphill battle, with the winner undecided but pessimistically evident.

Known for many years as the New Palace Diner, Jay bought the diner in 2003 from Stephen Prescott, who ran it under the name Justin Time Diner. Jay renamed it Cassidy's Diner after his son. The sign maker misspelled the name as "Cassidies," but the error stuck, and the diner unofficially goes by the erroneous spelling. Initially, the success of the diner was a textbook trend line going upward as daily revenues increased geometrically. "Meriden is still a beautiful city, and I love the people," said Jay, "but business has been in a steady decline for years. This is the worst economy I can remember. The downtown area and offices that sustained me have declined visibly, and people have no money to eat out. I get a little extra business when people cash their unemployment checks, but not much. Meriden is like a graveyard, and when you look at the faces of the people who used to eat here, they look like ghosts of their former selves." Jay even took a part-time job in an attempt to help defray expenses, but the gap between cost and profitability kept widening.

It isn't just the economy that's had a deleterious impact on Cassidy's Diner. In 2008, a woman who was simultaneously driving and breast-

Top: Cassidy's Diner owner Jay Eagle Delaney.

Left: Cassidy's Silk City plaque.

Below: Cassidy's Diner exterior.

feeding her infant drove her car right through the front of the diner. Jay wanted to restore the diner to its original form, but the insurance company was bent on replacing it, so a long, drawn-out battle ensued, with the result that Jay reopened, absorbing the cost of the repairs on top of an already weighty mortgage. Taking a second mortgage out to help defray repair costs brought him heavier into a debt that far exceeds the diner's appraisal value, making it unattractive to potential buyers. Cassidy's Diner is in a classic "rock and a hard place" spot.

Cassidy's Diner is considered "closed," but the door is open, and you'll find Jay inside, helping to provide meals to people in need, never considering himself needy but rather always looking out for someone else. "If anyone needs a meal or needs to talk, I'm here," offered a tearful Jay. "I'm serving coffee and making blueberry pancakes, bacon and eggs, toast, cheeseburgers and French toast. There are people who depend on me to be here. I haven't removed all the booths yet, and you can still sit at the stools." Vincent J. Gardon, founder and trustee of the Americans with Pancreatitis Foundation (AWPF), attested to Jay's community spirit and how he was there when the foundation's headquarters were being remodeled but succumbed to a fire that destroyed the facility just before opening. "Jay was there for us in spite of his own losses, and he is one of the main people in my life I can thank for keeping us going despite terrible loss and hardships. He is the reason we are still able to offer services and to keep the property afloat. I have learned what true compassion and brotherhood are from Jay, and I could never begin to repay him for his continued support. Even though he has lost everything, he encourages us to go on. We will continue to fight to help others in all walks of life as taught to us by a man of little wealth but great knowledge, compassion and spirit."

Jay symbolizes the core ingredient of classic diners: compassion for others. If you're ever tempted to determine whether a diner is a "classic" purely by the brightness of its neon, the authenticity of its terrazzo floors or the preservation of its porcelain flutes, go deeper to where the spirit meets the bone. Have a cup of coffee and talk about life with Jay Eagle Delaney. You will come to a place where "classic" has its most significant meaning.

TONY'S DINER
46 COLUMBUS STREET, SEYMOUR
CIRCA 1954 KULLMAN

In November 1955, the Connecticut Flood Recovery Committee released a summary report that noted, "Connecticut was the hardest hit victim of the worst flood in the history of the eastern United States." It was, in fact, a double hit of two major floods, one on August 19 followed by another on October 16.

On August 13, Hurricane Connie dropped almost six inches of rain on Connecticut. Less than a week later, Hurricane Diane layered an additional fourteen inches of rain on top of the already saturated landscape in only thirty hours. Connecticut residents pummeled by the first flood had barely recovered when the second flood devastated the already tragic scene left by gale winds and high tides. Connecticut was declared a disaster area on both occasions by then president Dwight D. Eisenhower, and then governor Abraham Ribicoff issued a statement on March 19, 1956, before the United States Appropriations Committee that quantified the extent of the tragedy:

- *91 persons dead and 12 others missing and presumed dead*
- *86,000 persons unemployed*
- *More than 1,100 families left homeless*
- *Another 2,300 families temporarily without shelter*
- *Nearly 20,000 families suffered flood damage*
- *Sixty-seven out of 169 towns were affected by the floods*

The damage to individual property, to business, to industry, and to State and municipal facilities has been estimated at almost half a billion dollars.

Tony's Diner survived the flood, but owners Tony and Carmella Librandi keep the photos of the damage close at hand to remind them to count their blessings and know that they have the fortitude to face anything together that might come their way. And they have had their share of challenges beyond the flood that confronted the former owners of the diner.

Tony's Diner, formerly Nash's Diner, then Joe's Diner and then the Seymour Diner, is a unique Kullman "dinette" produced in response to the wave of GIs returning home from World War II. Sitting under the Route 8 overpass down the street from the still operating 1941 698-seat Strand

Left: Tony's Diner outside.

Below: Tony's Diner owners Tony and Carmella Librandi.

Tony's Diner inside.

Tony's Diner during the 1955 flood, when it was originally called Nash's Diner.

Theater, Tony's Diner boasts a pride that spreads into the historic mill town community beyond its mere eleven stools and four booths. The diner has undergone restoration, and its stainless steel still shines brightly. Although the interior is faux wood paneling, it is nonetheless a step back in time, where the heart of a true diner continues to beat in spite of an elephant economy sitting on its chest. "The economy has hurt us," reflected Tony. "Business is not nearly what it used to be, but the regulars continue to come in, and the locals like to congregate here. Carmella and I raised our son, Mark, and our daughter, Daniela, here. They used to sleep in the booths. Now they help out." Daniela added, "It's where I've been since I was four. Now, at twenty, I work there on weekends."

Tony and Carmella greet patrons with a smile and are always available to talk about whatever's on their minds. The menu is basic diner fare with Italian specials. Tony's Special omelette, composed of eggs, bacon, onion, roasted peppers and cheese, is a frequent request, as is the Texan omelette of eggs, cheddar cheese, steak, chili, green peppers and onion. The other omelettes are contrasts: the meat lover's omelette contains ham, bacon, Italian sausage and cheese, while the veggie omelette has mushrooms, onions, peppers, tomatoes and cheese. Ham, mushrooms, onions, peppers and cheese compose the western omelette, while the eastern omelette is very similar to its western counterpart except that mushrooms are not included in the ingredients. The Country Kitchen omelette has potatoes with ham, onions and cheese. There are eleven additional omelettes rounding out the offerings. Blueberry pancakes, chocolate chip pancakes and French toast are standards on the menu. Ten breakfast sandwiches round out the breakfast menu, of which the standout is the Hottsie Sandwich, with egg, bacon, potatoes, chili and cheese.

The burgers at Tony's Diner are among the best I've ever had. "We pride ourselves on having the freshest and the highest-quality ingredients we can," declared Tony proudly. "People can taste when they're getting their money's worth. If someone doesn't like the food, he may not tell you, and you may never see him again. A diner owner can't take that chance. Every meal, no matter how simple or complex, has to be the best we can possibly make it. You can never take a customer for granted. Something as simple as a hamburger is what diners are known for. If we serve a customer the best hamburger around, they will probably come back." I often go to Tony's Diner just for the chili dog.

Italian cooking purists will find no compromises with any of the specials prepared by Tony and Carmella. I often check to find out if one of their

Italian specialties is being offered that day. So, the next time you have a craving for a *real* diner hamburger or delicious blueberry or chocolate pancakes, look for the patriotic red, white and blue sign at Tony's Diner and treat yourself to a bit of local history and a whole lot of home cooking. Tony will be glad to show you his historic photos, too.

GEORGIE'S DINER
427 ELM STREET, WEST HAVEN
1957 DeRAFFELE

Brother and sister Nicolas and Georgette Anthis are part of the new generation of classic diner owners. While most offspring of diner parents pursue careers outside the food industry once their parents have fulfilled their own dreams of giving their children a broader spectrum of opportunities than they had, Nicolas and Georgette are right at home managing their father's culinary legacy. "My dad, George, retired as a motorcycle policeman in Greece after fifteen years of service," Nicolas proudly shared, "and he and my mother decided to come to America. My Uncle John had already been running a diner called the Westporter, where my father worked and learned the business. When Georgie's Diner came up for sale in 1971, my father and uncle bought it. Not long after, my uncle decided to pursue another business, so my father ran the diner until 1988, when he retired and rented the diner. The tenant did not maintain Georgie's Diner, and it progressively went into serious disrepair. When the physical condition of the diner became critical, my father did not renew the lease and decided to restore it."

As Georgette recalled, "When we were faced with losing the tenant and having to fix the place up so we could find a new tenant, we realized how much Georgie's Diner was part of us as a family. We wanted to continue it ourselves because we knew no one but us could care for it as we would. We grew up in the diner. The help were our baby sitters. Our childhood is interwoven with the diner, as are our memories of growing up." Nicolas remembered his first job there: "I started working in the diner when I was six years old washing dishes. I had to stand on a milk crate to reach the sink."

More than the title to the diner passed hands from George to Nicolas and Georgette. "Everything our father did—coming to this country, making sacrifices, working hard—motivates us every day to keeping the diner running as he wanted it to. I'm very proud of my father," said Georgette, beaming. "He started from scratch and is a true success story. He changed countries as well as careers at an early age with a six-year-old and a baby to boot and made a life for himself and his family in America." Nicolas and Georgette have also been influenced by their father in becoming the personality of the diner, both at Georgie's Diner (named after their father) in West Haven and the Shoreline Diner in Guilford, which the two siblings also own. Nicolas fondly recalled how being social was a hallmark of the days when George was a policeman in Greece: "My father would always socialize with the residents and the business owners when he was patrolling. Often he would forget his gun. Nobody could have cared more for the people in his charge than my father. And no one was more perfect as a host in a people-business like running a diner."

Georgie's Diner itself, like George Anthis, moved to West Haven. Built in New Rochelle, New York, by the DeRaffele Manufacturing Company, the futuristic-looking diner was first situated in Stratford, where it was called the Duchess Diner. Then, in 1967, it was moved to its current location in West Haven. A beautiful neon sign captures the eye and almost hypnotically moves it toward the original stainless steel exterior, pulling your vehicle into the parking lot like a tractor beam. The inside glistens and shines, with light reflecting off the original ceiling as one gazes up, standing on the original terrazzo flooring, an incidental portion of which has been epoxied for repair purposes. A section of the original counter has been removed to accommodate more seating as demand for the tasty treats at Georgie's Diner has grown. The stools are new, but the kick plates and bases are original. For me, one of the most important attractions is the grill, which is located right behind the counter so you can engage the cook and your neighbors in conversation while your food is being prepared, and you can listen to and inhale the short-order cooking activity taking place directly in front of you.

Nicolas and Georgette have preserved the look, the activity and the social buzz of a classic diner while bringing the food into the twenty-first century. As Nicolas pointed out, "You have to preserve the structure, the environment of a classic diner. You want patrons to walk in and feel like they've stepped back in time. But when you order from the menu and your food comes out, you don't want some of the ingredients to be the same as back in the '50s. Food consciousness has increased dramatically the past few years. Nutrition is on everyone's mind. You wouldn't dare cook potatoes in lard anymore!"

For breakfast, you can build your own omelette at Georgie's Diner, with ingredients including bacon, ham, sausage, avocado, broccoli, mushrooms, onion, peppers, spinach, tomato, cheeses (American, cheddar, feta, Swiss, Manchego or gruyere) and eggs or egg whites. Or you can select from the assortment of thirteen omelettes on the menu, served with home fries, grits, sliced tomatoes or fresh fruit salad. There are several types of eggs Benedict, each one a feast in itself: the Classic (poached eggs and Canadian bacon on an English muffin topped with Hollandaise sauce), the Americana (sans the Canadian bacon), the New Yorker (smoked bacon and poached eggs on a toasted bagel topped with dill Hollandaise sauce), the Crabcake (crab cakes and poached eggs on an English muffin topped with cayenne Hollandaise) and the California (tomato, avocado and poached eggs on an English muffin topped with Hollandaise sauce). With all egg offerings, you can upgrade to organic eggs for a small extra charge.

The bagels are made in-house at Georgie's Diner, and you can have a plain one with cream cheese, smoked salmon or both or a full bagel deluxe platter with smoked salmon, cream cheese, capers, red onion, lettuce, tomato and lemon. Low-fat cream cheese, sugarless jam and reduced sugar spreads are available for the calorie watchers. You can sip a cranberry hibiscus mimosa with your breakfast for an extra-special touch. You have the option of a short or tall stack of pancakes to which you can add chocolate chips, blueberries or banana. There are buckwheat pancakes; Georgie's pancakes, with banana in the batter and topped with strawberries; French toast made from challah bread baked in-house; a Belgian waffle; or the Venetian waffle with ice cream, strawberries, banana, whipped cream and chocolate sauce, with the option to add chocolate chips or blueberries to the batter. Vegans can delight at the southwestern frittata, composed of tofu scrambled eggs with peppers, mushrooms and onion and topped with sliced avocado. It comes served with chips and salsa, and you can have as a side order pita bread, tofu or tempeh.

The menu at Georgie's Diner also boasts an array of vegan and gluten-free choices prepared in separate fryers and made under the strictest GFRAP guidelines. The owners have switched to canola oil in the fryer and on the griddle in response to the growing number of guests allergic to soy. And Georgie's Diner is now serving Five Acre Farms "Positively Local" milk and cream produced and sourced within 275 miles from where it is sold; it also has no added hormones.

As vast as the breakfast menu is at Georgie's Diner, the Georgie's Specialties always grab my attention. Maya's Breakfast is two pieces of challah French toast stuffed with a low-fat cream cheese filling and served with fresh kiwi, strawberries and maple syrup. The banana stuffed French toast is built on top of the house-made challah bread and stuffed with

Georgie's Diner owners Georgette and Nicolas Anthis.

Georgie's Diner outside.

Georgie's Diner sign.

Georgie's Diner inside.

caramelized bananas and topped with pastry cream. The caramelized apple French toast also uses the challah bread and is stuffed with caramelized apples and dusted with cinnamon sugar, with all of it topped off with a dollop of fresh whipped cream. The A.M. Cannolis are two pancakes rolled and stuffed with cannoli cream and dusted with powdered sugar. The butternut squash hash and eggs is composed of house-made butternut squash hash and potato hash seasoned with shallots, garlic and sage and all served with two eggs, home fries and toast. And this is just a partial list of Georgie's Specialties.

As for lunch at Georgie's Diner, you can select an alternative chicken, lamb, salmon, turkey or veggie burger, though for traditional burger holdouts, there is the eight-ounce Pat LaFrieda burger featuring a blend of prime chuck, shoulder and brisket that will raise the bar of expectations, as will the gourmet burger topped off with portobello mushrooms and tasty gorgonzola. Diner traditionalists will savor the home-style meatloaf.

Nestled under the shadow of the once-thriving Armstrong Factory that used to funnel lines of third-shift workers into Georgie's Diner—as did Sikorsky, which used to have facilities in West Haven, and Bayer Healthcare, which sold most of its local acreage and buildings to Yale University—the "little diner that could" keeps moving up the hill of economic change and challenge. "Georgie's Diner continues to have an interesting clientele," Nicolas pointed out. "Regular customers continue to come in, often more than once a day. They have become part of the Georgie's family, and as you know, it's always hard to leave home. Sometimes they just come in for a cup of coffee and to talk. We also serve travelers coming off of nearby Interstate 95 and families from out of town visiting students at the University of New Haven and Yale University." Just as it was growing up at home, good home cooking will always bring "family" members back to visit.

TOWER GRILL
185 FREIGHT STREET, WATERBURY
1955 BUILT ON-SITE

The city of Waterbury is located adjacent to the Naugatuck River, thirty-three miles southwest of Hartford and seventy-seven miles northeast of New

York City. As of the 2010 census, it is the ninth-largest city in New England, the fifth-largest city in Connecticut and the second-largest city in New Haven County. At ninety minutes from Manhattan, Waterbury is considered part of the New York Metropolitan Area. The city is located along Interstate 84 and Route 8 and has a Metro-North railroad station with connections to Grand Central Terminal.

Throughout the first half of the twentieth century, Waterbury was a major industrial player and the leading center in the United States for the manufacture of brassware, including castings and finishings, garnering it the appropriate nickname of "Brass City." Waterbury's factories provided the brass and copper used in constructing the Boulder Dam in Nevada, and its brass was also used in minting discs for nickels and in making South American coins. Another famous Waterbury product from the mid-nineteenth century was Robert H. Ingersoll's one-dollar pocket watch, of which 5 million were sold, making the clock industry as important as Waterbury's famed brass industry. One need only take a ride through the city among its many clock towers and historic factories to get a sense of just how productive Waterbury was at its manufacturing peak.

Providing warm meals to the factory workers was the Tower Grill, a family-owned and family-operated diner that has been a Waterbury landmark for more than fifty years. "My father, Steve Cotsoradis, was your typical Greek diner owner," explained son and current owner-operator Pete Cotsoradis. "He had a diner in Queens, New York, that he bought in 1967 originally called the Junction Diner and then the Olympic Diner. After twenty years running that diner, he wanted a change of scenery since the area was getting overcrowded and congested in Queens. He found the Tower Grill for sale in Waterbury and bought it, and we moved to a new beginning."

Pete was destined to become the next generation in Tower Grill owners. "I was born into the diner business. My mother, you might say, was waiting on tables and washing dishes while she was rocking me with one foot." The Tower Grill serves the usual diner fare. As Pete put it, "Diner food has to be three things: fast, affordable and good." Breakfasts are exceptional, and the coffee is superb. "Our coffee is excellent," boasted Pete, justifiably. "We use a process called 'full extraction,' so it doesn't get watered down. And we still make it in antique urns. You don't see many of those around!" Proper brewing of coffee requires using the correct amount of coffee grounds, extracted to the correct degree (largely determined by the correct time) at the correct temperature. Extraction involves what's called "solubles yield"—what percentage (by weight) of the grounds are dissolved in the water. The ideal yield is widely agreed to be 18–22 percent, as originally computed by the Coffee Brewing Institute under the direction of Professor E.E. Lockhart at MIT in the 1950s and which has been verified by subsequent tests by the Specialty Coffee Association of America. The usual ratio of coffee to water for the style of coffee most prevalent in Europe, America and other westernized nations is between one and two tablespoons of ground coffee per six ounces of water; the full two tablespoons per six ounces tends to be recommended by experienced coffee lovers. But the science behind coffee extraction is secondary to having that first morning cup of joe at the Tower Grill, when suddenly all's right in the world. And you can take that experience up several notches by having a slice of one of the homemade pies made by Polly, Pete's mom. She makes them on-site, and the aroma when they come out of the oven is hypnotic.

The exterior of the Tower Grill hasn't changed much since Steve Cotsoradis bought the diner in 1989. In the '70s, it underwent a makeover when Formica was installed over the counters, and the original tile flooring was covered over due to wear. In the restrooms, you can still see what the original black-and-white tile squares looked like, and behind the counters, the original wood flooring is evident. The seventeen stools and fifteen booths are original but have been re-covered. The diner took its name from the clock tower that looms over the city and is part of Union Station, which houses the Metro-North railroad and the *Republican-American* newspaper. The brick landmark, built by the Seth Thomas Company, is visible from the surrounding roads and highways like a huge compass needle and dates back to the first decade of the twentieth century.

Although Waterbury's motto, *Quid aere perennius?* ("What Is More Lasting than Brass?"), has a "last forever" optimism to it, the reality has been anything but positive. At its peak during World War II, ten thousand people worked at the Scovill Manufacturing Company, later sold to Century Brass. The city's metal manufacturing mills (Scovill Manufacturing, Anaconda American Brass and Chase Brass & Copper were the largest) occupied more than 2 million square feet and more than ninety buildings. Now, Waterbury is but a shadow of its formerly prosperous self. But the Tower Grill keeps on keeping on, in spite of its dwindling number of older patrons and the former 'round-the-clock factory operations no longer being a cacophony of sounds and workers filling the assembly lines and overflowing into the streets. Rather, it resembles one of those antique hand-tinted postcards hearkening back to better times. For customers visiting the Tower Grill, the homemade food

Tower Grill exterior.

Tower Grill owner Pete Cotsoradis.

Tower Grill dining area.

is hot and served in ample portions, just the way it satisfied the appetites of droves of third-shift workers from the nearby factories. When you arrive in the parking lot and look up at the clock tower, experiential time stops. But the quality of the food, the excellent service and Pete Cotsoradis's always-friendly greeting continue at the Tower Grill.

Hartford County

Hartford County is located in the central part of Connecticut and is home of the state capital. The county is laced with a network of major highways (I-91 and I-84) and major routes (Route 2, Route 15 and Route 44). Since there are no county-level executives or legislative governments in Connecticut, each city or town is responsible for its own local services, such as schools, snow removal and police and fire departments. While it is within the ability of cities and towns to provide combined services or a regional school system, the independence of each area lends itself to a feeling of local pride and community togetherness, a sentiment that is the perfect platform for such classic diners as Plainville's Main Street Diner, a 1950s Master-built gem; the Makris Midtown Diner in Wethersfield, produced in 1951 by O'Mahony; New Britain's circa 1962 "Princess" model Miss Washington Diner from the '60s Kullman production line; West Hartford's quaint, 1931 Quaker Diner, built on-site; and the iconic Olympia Diner in Newington, built by O'Mahony in about 1955, with its gleaming rooftop neon sign that has been the subject of countless photographs, paintings and drawings.

MAIN STREET DINER
40 WEST MAIN STREET, PLAINVILLE
CIRCA 1950 MASTER

Originally located on Main Street in Hempstead, Long Island, the Main Street Diner was relocated to its current address on West Main Street in Plainville. The beautiful neon sign that sits atop this gleaming landmark was never changed to reflect its "West" Main Street location.

Originally a farming, milling and small industrial town, Plainville struggled to realize its full economic potential because of the lack of good roads and dependable transportation. With the construction of the Farmington Canal in 1828, seventy-foot-long freighters shipped goods like tin ware, copper ore and timber from New Haven to Northampton, Massachusetts, while smaller freighters carried passengers and smaller products. Now Plainville's goods were on the move, and businesses expanded in size and variety, especially when the Farmington Canal was transformed into a railroad. Trains were faster and larger and drew large crowds of passengers while also hauling freight to destinations that the ships simply couldn't reach. In response to the financially unsuccessful canal, the New Haven and Northampton Company was built along the canal's right-of-way in 1848. The railroad merged with the New York, New Haven & Hartford Railroad in 1887, and portions of the railway were in use up until the 1980s. A two-mile section running from the Main and Whiting Streets intersection in downtown Plainville to just south of Townline Road is still in use, and memories of the historic railroad glory days can be felt as one sits in the Main Street Diner lying adjacent to the railroad tracks.

Just as trains have been a theme in both traditional and popular music since the first half of the nineteenth century, appearing across all music genres, Pam (the "singing waitress") is the face as well as the voice of the Main Street Diner. Always ready to take requests and lead a sing-along with the customers, Pam comes alive when she turns on the music player and serves orders with her own brand of impromptu karaoke. "The entertainment is free, as is the abuse," she jokingly offers. "I just charge you for the food." A classic diner waitress, Pam rides a Harley-Davidson Softail to work and reminisces as she dismounts about how her relationship with the diner came about. "I came along with the diner when the current owners, Frank and Kathy Loukoumis, bought it. You might say I was 'grandmothered' in."

The Main Street Diner serves up a classic diner experience with amazing food at good prices in an authentic vintage ambiance. Embraced by its stainless steel gleaming from all around and the thematic railroad lighting, patrons can choose from an assortment of homemade American diner plates served in generous portions. One day, when I had just sat down in a booth and picked up the menu to see what I would order, the radio started playing "Land of a Thousand Dances," a song written and first recorded by Chris Kenner in 1962. The song is famous for the "na na na na na" hook that Cannibal & the Headhunters added in their 1965 version, which reached number thirty on the Billboard chart. The "na na na na na" was added quite by accident when lead singer Frankie "Cannibal" Garcia forgot the lyrics. As I opened to the first page of the Main Street Diner menu, I couldn't resist relating the thirty-two omelettes listed to the song being played. I turned the menu around so Nanci Fox could see it from the other side of the booth, and I pointed, saying to her, "Look, land of a thousand omelettes!" She smiled back that tolerant smile she learned over time that signaled that she was accepting my often oddball attempts at humor. At least that day I spared her from what can be an endless stream of breakfast puns. Needless to say, in spite of there not literally being a thousand omelettes, neither did "Land of a Thousand Dances" actually mention that many dances. In fact, the song lyrics included only sixteen, half the number of Main Street Diner omelettes: the Pony, the Chicken, the Mashed Potato, the Alligator, the Watusi, the Twist, the Fly, the Jerk, the Tango, the Yo-Yo, the Sweet Pea, the Hand Jive, the Slop, the Bop, the Fish and the Popeye. Here are my sixteen Main Street Diner omelette faves:

- Florentine: spinach, tomatoes and mozzarella
- Brazilian: hot sausage, tomatoes, peppers, onions and melted cheddar cheese topped with salsa
- Hampton: broccoli, tomatoes, bacon and American melted cheese
- Popeye: spinach, sausage, mushrooms and melted mozzarella cheese
- Italian: sausage, peppers, tomatoes and melted mozzarella cheese
- Mexican: sausage and melted cheddar cheese topped with salsa
- Philly Steak and Cheese: Philly steak with peppers, onions and mushrooms
- Greek: feta cheese, tomatoes, spinach and olives
- Piggly Wiggly: bacon, ham, sausage and melted mozzarella cheese

- French: ham, potato, onion and melted Swiss cheese
- Grilled Chicken Cobb: grilled chicken, bacon and melted cheddar cheese
- Country: bacon, sausage, potato, onion and cheddar cheese
- Polish: kielbasa, peppers and melted Swiss cheese
- Hillbilly: ham, sausage, potato and melted American cheese
- Cowboy: ham, sausage and bacon topped with Hollandaise sauce
- Aspen: ham, peppers, onion and tomatoes

You'll have to visit the Main Street Diner to find out what the other sixteen omelettes are, but it will be well worth the trip ("na na na na na na na!").

For a different breakfast spin, you can try the turtle pancakes, with walnuts and chocolate chips; the nutty raisin pancakes, with walnuts and raisins; the Oreo cookie pancakes; or the ole standby, a short or tall stack of golden brown pancakes. There's also an assortment of French toast styles, of which my favorite is the cinnamon raisin. There are also four eggs Benedicts. The Eggs Mulligan is a Main Street Diner mainstay composed of two poached eggs with corned beef hash on an English muffin topped with Hollandaise sauce and served with home fries. The deep-fried country steak—smothered with gravy, topped with two eggs any style and served with toast and home fries—is worth not eating for the rest of the day. Those more culinarily conservative can select from the Healthy Heart menu section of low-carb scramblers and wraps. Biscuits are synonymous with Main Street Diner breakfasts, and like everything else, there are choices: buttermilk biscuits with country gravy, buttermilk biscuits deluxe, country sausage biscuits and crab cake biscuits. As Carl Sandburg once said, "Poetry is the synthesis of hyacinths and biscuits."

Hang on to the menu even after you've ordered breakfast. You owe it to yourself to take a glimpse at the lunch menu items to prepare you for your next visit. There are thirteen busting-at-the-seams deli sandwiches, four parmigiana sandwiches and twelve-inch hot dogs with optional add-ons of sauerkraut, onions, melted American cheese and bacon. The "sweet sixteen" classic sandwiches cover the menu roadmap of classic diner fare, although I've been known to ride considerably out of my way to have the Crabby Crab Melt of two crab cakes topped with Hollandaise sauce, roasted red peppers and melted American cheese on rye bread. The hamburger so associated with diner fare is exceptional at the Main Street Diner, but as you've probably gleaned by now, there's never just one at the MSD. There are almost a dozen

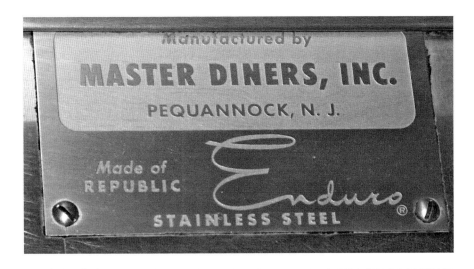

Above: Main Street Diner exterior.

Top: Main Street Diner Master Diners plaque.

Opposite, top: Main Street Diner exterior as seen from the railroad tracks.

Opposite, bottom: Main Street Diner interior.

and a half variations of the basic hamburger, of which the BBQ cheddar burger and the hot sausage burger stand out from the crowd for me. There are enough varieties of fresh garden salads to deplete the largest vegetable garden and fourteen wraps to wrap your hunger around, as well as an even dozen variations on the grilled chicken sandwich theme.

Dinner, you ask? Get ready for this roster: roast tom turkey with stuffing, Yankee pot roast, rib eye steak, wiener schnitzel, clam strips, Tuscan grilled chicken, pasta Bolognese, New England fish and chips, flounder, scallops, crab cakes and the list just goes on and on.

You may have missed the opportunity to catch a ride on the railroads that once frequented Plainville, but you don't need to miss out on the Main Street Diner experience. There's always a place for the hungry traveler to stop in, join the conversation, sing along with Pam and catch up with the past.

MAKRIS MIDTOWN DINER
1797 BERLIN TURNPIKE, WETHERSFIELD
1951 O'MAHONY

The motto of the town of Wethersfield is, "Ye most auncient town in Connecticut," and part of that legacy is the bragging rights to one of the best-preserved O'Mahony diners around: the Makris Midtown Diner. The original nameplate proudly hangs over the front entrance, beckoning hungry patrons in to a bit of history and a whole lot of great home cooking.

An immigrant from Poland in 1995, owner Eva Nowak came to the United States with an open mind and plenty of ambition—only she wasn't initially sure where to direct all of her boundless energy. Serendipitously, while pumping gas at the local fill-up, she ran into a friend she hadn't seen in a while who was making several trips back and forth to her car carrying bags of ice. Curious, Eva asked her what was going on. "I own a restaurant nearby, and we're short of ice. By the way, if you or anyone you know is looking to get into a business, the diner is for sale," her friend replied. After two years of wondering how she was going to spend her life, the friend's message caught her like an arrow on a targeted trajectory. She wrote down the name and address of the diner, as well as the phone number of her friend, and promised to let her know if she ran into any interested prospects, knowing full well that something was already piquing her curiosity.

The very next day, Eva was standing in the parking lot of the Makris Midtown Diner, allowing herself the full experience of falling in love at first sight. But unlike ancient odes of unrequited love, she bought the diner without hesitation and embarked on her adventure into classic dinerdom. Her pride in ownership was matched by the pride with which she took control of the kitchen and began to change the preparation of the food. As if in homage to fellow Wethersfield resident Tom Tryon's book title, *The Wings of Morning*, she's breathed new life into breakfasts at the Makris, with offerings that seem to reflect the pride in her creations, such as the Hearty Makris, the Mighty Makris and the Big Breakfast Special.

And there's no guilt in having Eva's incredible homemade corned beef hash with or without onions, even though Wethersfield was dubbed "Oniontown" in recognition of its being at the center of the onion trade in New England for a century. Eggs Benedict and the Monte Cristo lead off the list of classic breakfasts, and there is a grand variety of pancakes, enough to challenge anyone's ability to settle on just one, including wheat, blueberry, apple walnut, chocolaty chocolate chip, fresh fruit and more. Coffee is a special treat, and it's not just because it's always fresh and hot. The coffee is specially made for the Makris Midtown Diner from Middle and Central American beans roasted by a local coffee maker and also packaged for sale at the diner as a take-home item not available anywhere else. There are always other standard diner fare items, like club sandwiches, Reubens, chili dogs, overstuffed grinders and many others sure to keep you coming back with prices that afford you the opportunity to become a regular.

Eva's philosophy about how to run a classic diner flows out of her actions as naturally as she pours a cup of freshly brewed coffee. During one of my visits, an older woman who is a regular customer of the Makris Midtown Diner came in right at closing. As if no operating hours existed, Eva welcomed her and escorted her to the nearest booth. After inquiring as to how she was, the woman told Eva that she was not feeling well and had just come from the doctor's. Although she and her staff had pretty much shut down the kitchen and put away the food, Eva asked her what she would like, prepared as she was to make anything for the woman. "I'll cook whatever it is you want—just name it," was Eva's invitation as she handed the woman a menu. The woman simply wanted an escape for a little while from her apparent ordeal and requested only a cup of coffee as a salve for how she was feeling. And Eva never rushed the woman, even though it was long after the posted closing time when she finished her coffee.

Makris Midtown Diner exterior.

Makris Midtown Diner's Jerry O'Mahony plaque.

"Diners are about family," Eva said to me after the woman had left. "I hope that a cup of coffee or bowl of my soup will make any one of my customers feel a little bit better when they come into the diner. It doesn't matter what time of day it is. Home is never closed, and families are not by appointment. I know that the diner is a business and that I have to be mindful about making a profit and making sure that I have some personal life after closing. But why not spend just the few minutes it takes to make someone feel special? Isn't that what we all want—you, me and everyone?" As for Eva's endless energy, she credited her customers: "It's like a circle going around. Everyone who comes into the diner gives me something positive—something that makes me feel special. My customers make it easy for me to smile."

MISS WASHINGTON DINER
10 WASHINGTON STREET, NEW BRITAIN
CIRCA 1962 KULLMAN

"My dad brought me to my first diner on my twelfth birthday," recalled Dan Czako. "It was the best part of my celebration that day. I remember watching the grill cook and being amazed at how he could keep track of so many things going at the same time without burning them or forgetting an order. Everything came out perfectly. My jaw was on the floor, and I thought to myself, 'I am going to have my own diner someday.'" In 1998, the opportunity to realize the dream of his youth made itself known, and Dan bought the Miss Washington Diner.

This wasn't just any diner. The Miss Washington is a Kullman classic. The structure is original, as is the foundation, but the roof has been replaced due to wear. Inside, the twenty-four stools and ten booths have been reupholstered, and newer countertops have been overlaid onto the originals, which still exist like buried treasure underneath. The gold Kullman Diner logo, with black "KD" lettering supported by a chevron, is embedded in the terrazzo flooring, a mixture of marble chips and colored epoxy that is installed as a liquid by pouring it into the space and given time to cure. Once the terrazzo has hardened, it is ground down to expose the interior of the marble chips among the colored matrix. The finishing process involves grinding the top layer of the surface with a machine and filling in the air pockets with grout.

Afterward, a polishing machine is used to buff the floor to a matte finish, and a penetrating sealer is immediately applied in order to close the pores in the surface of the floor. In the Miss Washington Diner, the terrazzo floor is the perfect backdrop for the Kullman logo. Over the entrance door is a Kullman Diner plated logo welcoming patrons into a bit of history and a bite of home cooking.

Dan is one of the new breed of diner owners who came to the profession driven by that first childhood impression of diners that never seemed to let go. For so many diner owners, that first experience ultimately moves them from a wonderful experience growing up to running their own diner businesses and turning their passions into realities. Like veterans of the trade, the youthful Dan instinctually gets what goes into turning a diner into a classic. He knows how much a part of the allure of classic diners is all about keeping as much of their history and décor preserved, as well as re-creating the diner experience every minute of every day with every order taken and served. The notion of the diner as "family" has not eluded Dan in spite of his young entrance into the running of a diner. He has repeated the orchestration of food on the grill like he first experienced in his youth, with a natural flair for managing lots of orders during busy weekend breakfasts while always managing to greet customers, many on a first-name basis. His father-in-law, Allen Gauthier, a former chemist at Pfizer, manages the on-site bakery and is the source of the hypnotic aromas coming out of his oven. There is an unmistakable charm watching Dan and Allen in action together as they bridge the bond between their two generations around the operation of the Miss Washington Diner. It's a dynamic that is readily evident in their instinctual communication with each other.

"The key to making good pancakes, making a good burger, making a good milkshake all comes from starting from scratch with the best wholesome ingredients available," Dan insightfully declared. And the menu is an invitation to validate what Dan asserts in each and every offering. One of his flagship meals of which he is most proud is the Miss Washington Monument, composed of four half-pound patties topped with bacon strips, American, Swiss, provolone and cheddar cheese, four onion rings, A1 sauce, lettuce, tomato and a pickle. If you can finish it in twenty minutes, it's on the house!

For early birds, the specials served from 6:00 a.m. to 10:00 a.m. Monday through Friday are the perfect way to start the workday at prices the fast-food chains would have to struggle to beat at the quality of the food served at the Miss Washington Diner. There is also an assortment of breakfast sandwiches, of which a standout item is the breakfast burger, made up of a hand-formed

Miss Washington Diner owner Dan Czako.

Miss Washington Diner exterior.

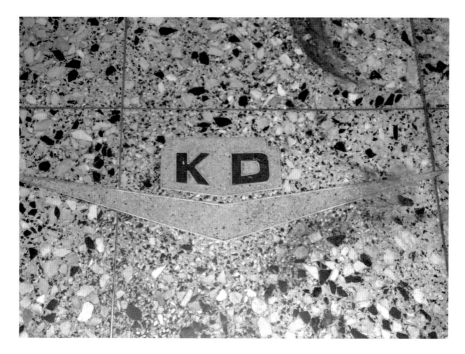

Miss Washington Diner Kullman Dining Car floor emblem.

Miss Washington Diner Kullman Dining Car plaque.

Miss Washington Diner interior.

patty (no assembly line burgers here), hash browns, fried eggs and American cheese served on an English muffin. The Hardware City is one of my favorites, with hash browns, kielbasa, Swiss cheese and sauerkraut. There are many omelettes to choose from, or you can build one from a list of delicious add-ons. Pay particular attention to the New Britski, made with kielbasa, sauerkraut, hash browns and Swiss cheese; the Texas omelette, composed of chili, cheddar cheese and your choice of raw or cooked onions; the Irish omelette, built around crispy corned beef hash and American cheese; and the Stanley Works, blending onions, peppers, mushrooms, tomatoes, ham, bacon, sausage and American cheese into a work of food art in homage to one of the region's largest companies.

The Miss Washington Diner menu lists eleven "Egg Breakfasts," including your basic one or two eggs any style with toast and home fries, as well as the optional bacon or sausage. From there, the list builds to a culinary crescendo as you explore such standouts as the New Englander (two eggs served with bacon, sausage, ham, home fries, toast and two pancakes with real maple syrup) and the Cowboy (eight-ounce sirloin steak, three eggs any style, home fries, toast and grits). There are very few places in this economy where you can get all-you-can-eat pancakes that also taste as good as the ones at the Miss Washington Diner. The stuffed French toast might be the only other griddle item on the menu that challenges the pancakes in your decision-making. My recommendation is to go with a group and taste samples of what each person orders so that you get a full idea of just how extensive and delicious the breakfasts are.

Diner traditionalists will find the basic hamburgers and cheeseburgers at the Miss Washington Diner excellent, topped off with French fries or onion rings. The bleu burger is especially delicious, as is the Reuben burger, with corned beef, sauerkraut, thousand island and Swiss cheese. There is an ample assortment of fully loaded grinders that overflow around the edges, as well as a complete selection of sandwich board offerings that are also available in wraps.

No matter what you order at the Miss Washington Diner, you can be assured that it will taste great and make your visit to this Kullman space-age "Princess" the best part of any day.

QUAKER DINER
319 PARK ROAD, WEST HARTFORD
1931 BUILT ON-SITE

When you sit at one of the seventeen stools or six booths at the Quaker Diner and pick up the small six- by nine-inch menu from between the napkin holder and the ketchup bottle, it speaks to the simplicity of this historic 1931 diner gem that was designed by a Hartford architect, built where it continues to sit today by a local construction company and outfitted by a local diner company. The cover of the menu proudly displays a photo of the original owner, Aristedes "Harry" Bassilakis, grandfather of the third-generation (and current) owner, Harry. The breakfast selection includes eggs, pancakes, omelettes, corned beef hash, sausages and muffins, standard diner fare served right from the grill behind the counter in helpings large enough to satisfy any appetite. Daily handwritten lunch specials are taped to the wall on sheets of paper, and I consider the pot roast the best I've ever had. Consider

Quaker Diner owner Harry Bassilakis.

yourself extra lucky on days when Michele Mancuso is your waitress. She never fails to greet every customer with a smile and friendly conversation. Michele has worked at the Quaker Diner in West Hartford, Connecticut, for twenty-three years. Her stepmother worked there when it opened, so diners are clearly in her family's DNA. She'll even offer you a sample of something on the menu if you're not sure what to order.

Harry's dream had always been to restore his grandfather's diner business, and he left a successful career in the insurance business to dedicate all of his time and resources to doing it right. The Park Road area was undergoing a major renovation, and because the Quaker Diner was deemed historically significant due to its age and architecture, it was eligible for extensive outdoor renovations by the Park Road Commission. The entire Bassilakis family was conscripted into service for the restoration, and they became amateur archaeologists, historians and craftspeople overnight, stripping countless layers of paint to bring the original green color back to life. The search went on to locate replacements for missing black and green floor tiles, which they then meticulously inserted among the original tiles. Like an episode in the life of Indiana Jones, they came across a small shard of the original china, and the search was on to find dishes that matched it.

Photos of the original Quaker Diner are proudly hung throughout the establishment, clustering most noticeably behind the cash register (they don't take credit cards). "Tom Robinson used to run the gas station next door. He'd watch his pumps looking out the diner window from the last stool at the counter," Harry pointed out. "And there used to be a trolley stop at the end of the street," he added, pointing in the direction of the original stop. "The trolley conductor would simply push the seats back so they faced in the opposite direction, then drive the other way. The original counter was glass and wood," he noted, pointing to a photo on the wall. "And it was refrigerated. Unfortunately, it had to be replaced. Customers originally paid for their meals with cardboard tags. The waitress would click twenty-five cents or ten cents, and the customer would bring the tag to the register to pay."

Harry likened the classic diner experience to a cafeteria. "Remember when you ate in the school cafeteria? Eating at a diner is just like that. You're with friends talking about all kinds of things that interest you." Just about to start his next sentence, Harry quickly got up from his stool at the counter where we were talking, excused himself and stated, "Wait, I want to show you something." He hustled downstairs to his basement office and returned with a file folder. From inside of it, he very carefully pulled out a handwritten letter from a woman who worked in a nearby factory during World War II and frequented the Quaker Diner from her apartment in the neighborhood. "This letter came to me in the mail," he said, gingerly handing me the letter as if placing a baby bird in my hand. "Here's what the diner experience is all about." Excerpts of what Harry wanted me to read are as follows:

In 1943, with World War II underway, I moved to CT to help with the war effort. After landing work at the Niles Bement Pond branch of Pratt & Whitney I rented a room and began looking for a breakfast spot. The Quaker Diner filled the bill and for the ensuing three years an extremely satisfying relationship flourished. Every morning at approximately 6:15 I entered the diner and by the time I found a seat at the counter Harry would have started preparing my poached egg, toast and coffee. As the years rolled by, Harry kept a watchful eye on me. Often, wordlessly, he would place the morning paper beside me. Sometimes, I would overhear him advising a male patron to give me his paper when finished with it. Every Saturday noon after work I had lunch at your grandfather's. He made me feel cared for and welcome.

Quaker Diner exterior.

Quaker Diner vintage exterior photo.

Quaker Diner vintage interior photo.

Harry turned silent as I finished reading the letter and handed it back to him, thanking him for sharing what was obviously something deeply meaningful to him. He held on to the letter for what seemed like minutes before returning it to the file folder, then got up without saying anything and walked head-bowed back to his office to restore the letter to what I'm sure is a coveted place in his desk. For Harry Bassilakis, the Quaker Diner is about all the things that make a classic diner what it is: good food served at fair prices by an attentive waitstaff that treats you like family. But at a much deeper level, the torch that was passed to him by his grandfather, Aristedes "Harry" Bassilakis, after whom he was named, is a legacy that defines family and how people should be treated. Harry's philosophy of life and how classic diners should be operated are inseparable. You won't find either on the menu. You need to experience what classic diners are all about by spending time at the Quaker Diner.

OLYMPIA DINER
3413 BERLIN TURNPIKE/ROUTE 5, NEWINGTON
CIRCA 1955 O'MAHONY

The Olympia Diner sits catty-corner facing the Berlin Turnpike, the bright neon glow of its huge diner sign atop the roof being its most well-known and distinguishing feature. Although it could be one of the largest Mahony-built diners, approaching the Olympia from the front, one has no clue just how big it really is inside. The front entrance brings you into the original part of the diner, with its 16 booths and 21 stools, impressive enough when it comes to the scale of diners from its era. However, in 1986, second-generation brother-owners Steve and Tasos Gavrilis expanded with an addition onto the back of the original diner, adding another 115 seats to the already impressive capacity. The expansion has enabled the Olympia Diner to accommodate its continually growing customers while keeping its original look and feel.

The exterior of the Olympia Diner is 100 percent original stainless steel, and the interior flooring is the original terrazzo, as beautiful and solid as the day it was installed. The booths are new, but the ambiance is the genuine diner experience. The Olympia Diner passed hands from Greek-born father Emmanuel "Manny" Gavrilis to his sons in 1974. Emmanuel learned the diner business starting as a dishwasher, working himself up to cook and then owner. His role model work ethic is a hallmark of the efforts that Steve and Tasos put into the diner to keep it looking and running like it does. "The Olympia Diner feels solid. It has a good foundation, and I don't mean just physically," commented Steve. "We have perfected the food and service of a successful Greek-run American diner. Nothing happens by chance. The food, the ingredients, the service, the atmosphere are well thought out. Nothing is left to chance in perpetuating the diner experience our father began. The diner was a second home to our father, and he considered many of his customers to be his friends. We honor him by continuing to manage the diner with the same attitude." Just in case, Florence Gavrilis, their mom, is often around working the register and keeping an eye on things.

The Olympia Diner used to serve customers 24/7, but when the clientele got too rowdy for the third shift and the economy didn't justify the additional operating hours, the Gavrilises made the decision to be open from 6:00 a.m. to midnight. Breakfasts are available anytime. Custom-made omelettes are a frequent request. You can create your own by choosing a single or several items (bacon, broccoli, tomato, sausage, spinach, ham, mushroom or onion)

Olympia Diner exterior.

and then get creative with additional meats, vegetables and cheeses. There are also the "prebuilt" western, Greek, cheese and Spanish omelettes. There is the basic diner breakfast of one, two or three eggs any style, with home fries and toast, and you can select a side order of bacon, ham, sausage, pastrami or corned beef hash. There are plenty of pancakes, with blueberry, chocolate chip, apple or strawberry toppings, as well as a Belgian waffle

with apple or strawberry topping and whipped cream and French toast. For hearty appetites, there's the hash and cheese omelette (stuffed with corned beef hash and served with home fries and toast), the Philly steak omelette (Philly steak, mushrooms, onion and cheese), the Olympian (corned beef hash, three eggs any style, home fries and two pancakes), steak and eggs (eight-ounce steak with two eggs any style, served with home fries and toast)

Olympia Diner owners Steve Gavrilis and his mother, Florence.

Olympia Diner interior.

and Virginia ham steak and eggs (thick ham steak with two eggs any style, home fries and toast).

Classic burgers and cheeseburgers are part of the standard diner fare at the Olympia, but you can take your burger experiences up several notches with their specialty eight-ounce burgers, including the European burger (seasoned with a special blend of herbs and topped with lettuce and tomato), the Olympia burger (with lettuce, tomato, crisp bacon and a slice of onion), the Philly cheeseburger (smothered in sautéed onions and mushrooms and covered with American cheese) and the turnpike burger (served with grilled onions and fresh roasted peppers, topped with bacon and American cheese and finished with a special sauce). From the grill, you can get your basic tuna melt, foot-long hot dog, BLT, hot pastrami or corned beef on rye, hot meatloaf, western sandwich or pot roast or roast pork sandwich. There are twelve hot oven grinders, triple-decker club sandwiches, an assortment of salads and cold platters and the massive Olympia sandwich platters, with a lineup that includes corned beef or pastrami, Philly steak, fried filet of sole, grilled chicken breast, Reuben, clam roll or fajita on a pita.

Dinners at the Olympia Diner are comfort food at its best, with such standard but wonderfully delicious menu items like Virginia-style ham steak, Yankee pot roast, fried chicken, baked meatloaf with gravy, roast stuffed chicken, beef liver, breaded pork chops, roast pork and roast stuffed turkey. You can go international from there and have Greek specialties like chicken or pork kabob, gyros or moussaka or take an Italian bent with veal cutlet parmigiana, baked lasagna, chicken parmigiana with pasta, meat or cheese raviolis, eggplant parmigiana with pasta, baked manicotti, spaghetti, ziti or shells or grilled chicken Alfredo. From the Olympic Diner broiler, there's twelve-ounce boneless rib eye steak, eight-ounce boneless sirloin steak, broiled boneless pork chops, broiled hamburger steak or broiled half chicken. For seafood lovers, there are broiled catches, including swordfish, filet of sole, salmon filet or baked stuffed filet of sole, or fried offerings like clam strips, crab cakes, sea scallops, filet of sole, shrimp and a combination sea platter.

Desserts are a must, and there are plenty to choose from: home-style fruit pies, cream pies, lemon meringue pie, cheesecake with fruit topping, brownies, carrot cake, German chocolate cake, classic rice pudding, chocolate pudding and the Olympia sundae made with three scoops, fruit, chocolate syrup and whipped cream. It can take a while to finish off the large quantities of food served at the Olympia Diner, but you can never argue that you're not getting your money's worth. And while you're eating your meal, there are jukeboxes at every booth, as well as Wi-Fi for those who want high-tech amenities with their classic diner experience.

Middlesex County

Middletown, the hub of Middlesex County, is sixteen miles south of Hartford and located on the Connecticut River, with easy access to major highways, airports, railroads and other modes of transportation. Originally a busy sailing port and industrial center, Middletown is now largely residential, with its downtown serving as a college town for Wesleyan University. Middlesex County has been the home of many well-known celebrities, including James Naughton (two-time Tony Award winner for his cynical, Sam Spade–like detective in *City of Angels* and slick, shyster lawyer/razzle-dazzler Billy Flynn in the revival of *Chicago*), Jules Dassin (Academy Award–nominated director, screenwriter and actor best known for his films *Rififi*, *Never on Sunday* and *Topkapi*), David Webb Peoples (writer, *Blade Runner*), Conor Timmis (actor, *The Mandala Maker*), Emily Johnson (actress, *Beowulf*), Nate Barlow (actor, *Tales from Beyond*), Allie Wrubel (soundtrack, *8 Mile*), Tim Pixton (visual effects, *The Incredible Hulk*) and so many others. But no local figure is more popular or more well known to residents of Middletown and beyond than Brian O'Rourke, owner of O'Rourke's Diner, a 1946 Mountain View that is synonymous with life along the Middletown Main Street.

O'ROURKE'S DINER
728 MAIN STREET, MIDDLETOWN
1946 MOUNTAIN VIEW #223

Main Street in Middletown, Connecticut, is no mere metonym or rhetorical figure of speech, although a photo of it could be the subject for any of illustrator Eleanor Campbell's *Dick and Jane* book covers or a premier addition to every deltiologist's collection of vintage postcards. One of the widest streets in Connecticut, it has been the main artery since 1650 of the city's economic, religious and community lifeblood alongside the Connecticut River, which brought world commerce to the town's shoreline. Anchoring the north end of Main Street, within eyeshot of the architecturally impressive twin structures of St. John's Roman Catholic Church and St. John's School, is O'Rourke's Diner.

Rich in its own history, O'Rourke's is one of the few diners built by the New Jersey–based Mountain View Diner Company, which is still operating today. Its birth certificate lists 1946 as its year of manufacture, and it wears its serial no. 223 proudly. Genealogically, O'Rourke's Diner is a direct descendant of its wooden predecessor, Dunn's Diner, which was purchased in 1941 by John O'Rourke, uncle to the current owner, Brian O'Rourke. Uncle John was part of the crew at Jack's Lunch, located at 434 Main Street. Steamed cheeseburgers kept Jack Fitzgerald's eatery busy with customers and his simmering copper box filled with square patties for forty-four years. Jack learned the trade from Spencer G. "Pop" Page, who, after unhitching his horse from his food wagon and sending it home on its own with a swat to the backside, ran an electric cable to the cart and sold hot sandwiches on Main Street in the late 1800s and early 1900s.

The "art of the cart" passed from "Pop" to Jack and then to Uncle John, who, after purchasing Dunn's Diner, satiated the demands of his increasing customer base by buying the Mountain View–manufactured diner in 1946 that resides today at 728 Main Street. The diner DNA passed to Brian from Uncle John, who as a youngster was assigned the task of bringing up supplies from the basement:

> *My beginning here was as a young boy. Across the street, I went to school at St. John School. We went to church every morning. We went to school every morning. And we went to the diner every morning. My father used to ring the bells at six o'clock mass, so after mass, we used to come over to the diner*

*and have toast and chocolate milk. As I got to be seven or eight years old,
there was always something needed upstairs. Everything was downstairs in
a walk-in. Back in the '50s, we got milk in six-ounce bottles. We got Coke
in six-ounce bottles. You got everything individualized, so there was a lot of
running. One day, I ran downstairs to get a case of Coke. The next day, I
ran downstairs to get two cases of Coke. The next day, I got milk and Coke.
After that, it was a bag of potatoes. By the time I was ten years old, I was
here every day of the week, peeling potatoes, washing dishes, and that was
the beginning of my involvement with the diner.*

By high school, Brian was working forty hours a week grilling eggs in
addition to delivering newspapers. Along with his cousin, John Sweeney
O'Rourke, Brian would ultimately purchase the diner from his retiring
Uncle John in 1977, taking full proprietorship in 1985.

Brian set the culinary stage for what would attract the praises of *USA
Today*, the *New York Times*, *Gourmet* and *Yankee*. He infused the menu with his
experiences in the kitchens of New Orleans, Ireland and the Caribbean and
reinvented the omelette. In fact, there is an entire page of the O'Rourke's
Diner menu dedicated to Brian's twenty omelette creations. Choosing which
one to order can be challenging, especially with such standouts as the Black
Forest (house-baked ham with Swiss cheese topped with bacon), Bob Wolfe's
(guacamole, tomato, provolone and bacon served with corned beef hash and
brown bread), Cajun firecracker (cheese, creole sauce, mushrooms, onions
and peppers topped with Andouille sausage), the Dubliner (corned beef hash
and Irish cheddar cheese served with Irish bacon, fingerling potatoes and
Irish soda bread topped with jam), the Salmon (asparagus, salmon, capers
and mushrooms) and all the other Brian O'Rourke creations that will dazzle
and amaze you, as well as satisfy your cravings for eggs-cellent omelettes.

And just when you thought you could take that deep breath of self-
achievement, having read about all of the "Omelettes by Brian," you turn
to the very next page and are held captive by the range of eggs Benedict
options. Of course there is the basic "EB," but that's only a jumping-off
point to such new classics as Brian's Eggs Oscar. The following is but a short
sample. Eggs Oscar is composed of poached eggs with Swiss cheese and
asparagus on an English muffin topped with Hollandaise sauce and served
with poached shrimp and fingerling potatoes. Irish Galway is composed
of poached eggs over grilled brown bread with smoked salmon and bacon
topped with Hollandaise sauce and served with home fries. And Irish
Embassy is composed of grilled bacon and poached eggs over brown bread

O'Rourke's Diner exterior.

O'Rourke's Diner owner, Brian O'Rourke.

O'Rourke's Diner interior.

topped with Hollandaise sauce and served with Irish bacon, home fries and your choice of corned beef or vegetable hash.

The rest of the eggs Benedict creations are equally amazing. If you really want to try something unique from the griddle, my recommendation is the Irish soda bread pancakes, topped with a variety of homemade jams and clotted cream, which were featured in *Connecticut* magazine's "Dishes to Try Before You Die" and in *Yankee* magazine. The banana bread French toast is also incredible, as is the Babka French toast.

For lunch, you can journey back in time and have a steamed cheeseburger, which has been famous since 1941. Or try the Kronenberger Steamer, named after Tom Sr., the patriarch of Kronenberger & Sons Restoration Inc., a three-generation firm founded in 1946 specializing in the restoration, preservation and adaptive reuse of period structures that helped oversee the post-fire restoration of O'Rourke's Diner. Specialty burgers are aplenty at O'Rourke's, as are the Reubens, my favorite of the latter being the 728 Main Street, made with corned beef, turkey, baked ham and Swiss cheese and served with sweet potato fries—it brings to my mind the J.R.R. Tolkien quote,

"If more of us valued food and cheer and song above hoarded gold, it would be a merrier world." Long after you've ordered and while you're waiting for your food to arrive, you'll still be reading from the menu's elaborate list of culinary delights. Brian himself is the "secret sauce" that ties all of the items on the eclectic menu together.

O'Rourke's Diner sits at its rightful place on Main Street, testament to the motto of its manufacturer: "A Mountain View Diner will last a lifetime." On August 31, 2006, the diner was decimated by a kitchen fire caused by a hamburger steamer that was left on overnight. Without any fire insurance to cover the estimated $350,000 repair tab, fundraising efforts were launched, and in less than a year, the $180,000 raised was enough to launch reconstruction. "Community" is one of the hallmarks of classic diners. In Brian's own words, "A diner is a way of life. It's a major part of the community," as demonstrated by the outpouring of support to make sure that O'Rourke's Diner retained its important place on Main Street. "I have a PhD in 'dinerology,'" he added. "Dinerology touches every aspect of life, anything and everyone you can imagine, from a motorcycle rider to a cheerleader to babies to schoolteachers to presidents. You name it, diners touch it. We are the biggest cross-section of life there is."

Litchfield County

F ounded in 1721, Litchfield was designated the county seat in 1751, and by the 1790s, the town had become the leading commercial, social, cultural and legal center of northwestern Connecticut, such that by 1810 Litchfield was the fourth-largest settlement in the state. The fifty years between 1784 and 1834 are known as Litchfield's "golden age." During these years, the town was an active, growing urban center. Local merchants made fortunes in the China trade, small industries were developed and by 1810 the central village contained 125 houses, shops and public buildings. The town had an active artisan community with goldsmiths, carpenters, hatters, carriage makers, joiners, cabinetmakers, saddlers, blacksmiths, potters and other craftsmen all located within the central village. During its "golden age," Litchfield had an unusual number of college-educated inhabitants. In 1791, Samuel Miles Hopkins, a student at the Litchfield Law School, described Litchfield in his journal as a town of "hard, active, reading, thinking, intelligent men who may probably be set forth as a pattern of the finest community on earth."

Reverend Dan Huntington, a Congregational minister in the town from 1798 to 1809, wrote upon his arrival in Litchfield, "A delightful village on a fruitful hill, richly endowed with schools both professional and scientific, with its venerable governors and judges, with its learned lawyers, and senators both in the national and state departments and with a population both enlightened and respectable, Litchfield was now in its glory." Litchfield's fortunes declined during the later years of the nineteenth century. The town did not have the ample water supply and rail transportation necessary to establish industry, and the village became a sleepy backwater community. Rediscovered as a resort community in the late nineteenth century, Litchfield became a popular spot for vacation, weekend and summer homes. The town embraced the Colonial Revival movement, and by the early century, many of the homes had begun to sport the white paint and black shutters that we see today.

Canaan is the second-smallest town in Litchfield County. In spite of its outward appearance of peacefulness, its history is anything but quiet. For it was here, beginning in the early eighteenth century, peaking in the nineteenth century and ending in the early twentieth century, that stone blast furnaces poured forth red-hot, high-quality Salisbury iron. Mountains and valleys were stripped bare of trees to make charcoal to feed the hungry furnaces. A huge factory once stood at the Great Falls and employed hundreds of men to manufacture cannons, war matériel and huge railroad wheels from the famed Salisbury iron. One hundred years ago, the center of town, now so quiet, was a beehive of commercial activity, a boomtown, and early entrepreneurs dreamed of channeling the power of the falls to fuel an industrial empire. Thankfully, the iron industry moved to the easily accessible surface iron mines of the Midwest, the plans for empire collapsed, the ravaged mountains and valleys reclaimed their natural splendor and the peaceful life of a small town returned. Today, the stunning and unspoiled natural beauty of Falls Village remains one of its most prized and closely guarded assets, and its rich New England heritage remains firmly in place guiding its future.

Among the most prized historical assets of Litchfield County are the O'Mahony-manufactured Collin's Diner, which stands as an ongoing, active testament to the golden age of diners, and the tiny, tucked-away Tierney-built Winsted Diner, which proves with every well-portioned, home-cooked meal that good, wholesome food will sell itself—it doesn't need Whopper-size marketing or Big Mac branding.

COLLIN'S DINER
728 MAIN STREET, NORTH CANAAN
1942 O'MAHONY

The food at the Collin's Diner doesn't pretend to be something it isn't. The menu is basic diner fare served within the walls of a wonderful diner-

Collin's Diner exterior.

Collin's Diner interior.

nostalgic structure, with cozy booths and counter service. The food is fresh and cooked to order without being overly complicated. It's all about the simplicity of eggs any style you want and burgers and fries. The front of the diner is replete with photos of politicians who love the diner and articles about the diner from renowned publications. Reading the wall, so to speak, gives one a real sense of the diner's history and the recognition that this historic eatery has garnered well beyond its regional location. The Collin's Diner has been a stopping place for persons traveling through the area on their way north or south from the Berkshires.

While the classic O'Mahony diner itself is not even a bit different structurally and aesthetically from when it was plopped on its cinder blocks more than seventy years ago, it has passed through different ownership and staffing through the years. Mike Hamzy originally bought the diner in 1970 and his wife, Aida, was the resident personality and face of Collin's. Patrons reminisce today about her conspicuous absence from the day-to-day chatter and goings-on. The diner is located in a designated historic district near the former New Haven Railroad station, so it benefits from the town's nostalgic air.

Winsted Diner
496 Main Street, Winsted
1931 Tierney

Beginning in February 1967, a decade-long series of separate UFOs sightings was reported in Winsted. One driver told police that he had been buzzed by a round, silver, dish-shaped object that caused the engine to seize and bring the vehicle to a stop. As the UFO passed overhead, he claimed that the door wouldn't budge when he tried to leave the car, and an object that looked somewhat like a camera (and might have taken his snapshot) appeared below the low-flying disc. UFO researcher Ted Thoben declared that the area of the town is one of two UFO windows in America, the other being the Michigan Rectangle. In all my rides through Winsted, my motorcycle does seem come to an almost uncontrollable stop when I reach the Winsted Diner, but I've yet to see any saucers other than the ones that have cradled my many cups of coffee as I devoured the signature Ra-Doc-a-Doodle sandwich composed of eggs, Tennessee sausage and American

Winsted Diner exterior.

Winsted Diner owner Asa Flint.

The original Winsted Diner site.

cheese. While some Winsteders claim to have been abducted by aliens and talk about entering an altered state of consciousness, locals will tell you that a few days without being "Doodled" can have a deleterious effect on anyone's culinary well-being.

There's a lot of "Rocky" in the town of Winsted and its cherished diner. Like the prizefighter who won't go down no matter what combination of punches you throw at him, the town and the diner got up from the canvas before the ten count of the 1955 flood from Hurricanes Connie and Diane, which caused the Mad River that parallels Main Street to flood more than twenty feet, causing all buildings on that side of Main Street to be removed. Farther downstream, the flooding Still River caused extensive local fires and the closing of major local employers like Gilbert Clock Company, which had become one of the largest clock companies in the world around the start of the twentieth century. The Main Street has refused to succumb to all the weather-related and economic challenges thrown at it. In fact, when crises in the town do occur, residents converge on the little eatery to ride out the storm, plug their cellphone chargers in and exchange comforting words surrounded by little signs reminding them to "Keep Smiling" and that "Life Is Good." It's the local version of the Beatles' "Penny Lane," with firemen coming in for a meal after extinguishing a fire, musicians extending a nearby rehearsal with eggs and an impromptu performance and craftsmen grabbing a bite between jobs.

The tiny Winsted Diner continues to take on the challenges of nearby fast-food giants McDonald's and Burger King, as well as the disappearance of third-shift factory workers. The diner seems even tinier when you sit at one of the little round discs that are the original fifteen stools obviously crafted to accept the backsides of customers who were then smaller-girthed patrons. There are no booths at the diner because there simply is no room for them. Asa Flint, a veteran of the food industry as a deli and bakery proprietor, has owned the diner for less than a year and runs it as a one-man show. "You can't have a lot of people working here," he said, pointing to the limited workspace. "You have to do it all by yourself. Thank goodness I'm fast enough so that I can." The Winsted Diner could be the location for an episode of *The Twilight Zone* about a business refusing to step out of history and frozen in time. "I still have the original phone number from 1931," said Asa, pointing to the number on the wall. "The locals are glad I'm open because they depend on me for a good home-cooked meal and a cup of coffee. But they don't have the jobs and the income they used to have to eat out often. Winsted is a dying town, and a classic diner needs its local customers to support it. I made it through the first year covering my bills and expenses, but I didn't take a paycheck for myself. I'm hoping I can grow the business and be able to make a profit, but we'll see. I can't do it by myself. The town simply has to rebound."

Breakfast items are the standout fare at the Winsted Diner. "Breakfasts are what diners are known for," a smiling Asa Flint declared, "but I also sell about thirty quarts of chili a week. I make it myself. My homemade corned beef hash is asked for a lot, as is my Cuban sandwich."

New London County

New London County is located in the southeastern corner of Connecticut, bordering Long Island Sound. The total area of the county is 772 square miles, including inland and coastal waters, and is served by several roadways, the most notable highway being Interstate 95. Jewett City, home of Charlene's Diner, became nationally well known when it was featured on *The Daily Show with Jon Stewart* after being at the center of a church bell controversy in a segment called "Sam on Your Side" about the ringing of the Jewett City bells.

Norm's Diner resides in Groton, a town located on the Thames River in New London County. The town is home to the Electric Boat Corporation, the major contractor for submarine work performed for the U.S. Navy and the largest employer in town. In 1954, Electric Boat launched the USS *Nautilus*, the world's first nuclear-powered submarine. The Naval Submarine Base New London is located in Groton, as is the pharmaceutical giant Pfizer.

CHARLENE'S DINER
37 MAIN STREET, JEWETT CITY
ORIGINAL CIRCA 1920 O'MAHONY

The power of home cooking and a personality focused on its patrons is what has kept customers coming to Charlene's Diner, even though it has moved from its original stand-alone structure at 53 Main Street to its current location at street level in an office building a little ways up at 37 Main Street. When Charlene Schultz purchased the original little Charlene's Diner, with its barrel-roof and weathered exterior, it was one of the oldest diners in Connecticut, but it was a new entrepreneurial venture for her.

"The original owners, Stanley and Lena Snide, sold the diner to Jimmy Tangway, and I bought it from him," Charlene shared. "I started working at the diner when I was sixteen. Back then, it was called Chick's Diner. I was a young mother and needed a job. Little did I know that as the years rolled by I would fall in love with diners to the point where all I could dream of was when I'd own it for myself." Taking the step of owning the diner was a big one for Charlene. Although she had worked there for many years before buying it, knowing how to waitress was different than owning the place. "I had no credit. I owned a home, which I used as equity. I was the only person working there. I took home sixty dollars on a good week and couldn't afford to hire anyone else. So, I waited, cooked and did the dishes. My original stove was four feet wide and had two burners. The original diner had ten stools, five booths and one tiny little table," she reminisced. "That original little table is over there by the door," Charlene said, pointing to its place at the entrance of the current diner.

Before moving to the new location in 2001, it was Charlene's intention to actually rebuild the original diner where it had been located. "When I bought the diner, it was in need of upgrading. In fact, I wanted to actually replace it with a bigger one, but I didn't own the land. On the other hand, I couldn't move too far away because of my customers who depended on me being open. When the new space became available up the street, I made the move since it already had meaning for me. I used to live in the building when I was first married and shop at the A&P and Montgomery Ward when they were there. There was even a theater upstairs."

That Charlene's Diner exists today is a lesson in survival that all small businesses can take note of and learn from.

Years ago, we used to be open until midnight when the mills were around. Now there's not much going on business-wise at night. I still get a lot of regular customers, and I treat them well and take care of them. That's the old-fashioned diner way. We've made a lot of sacrifices over the years, but the rewards have been enormous, and you can't always measure them by profits. The people connections are what are most important—caring for each other and looking out for each other. The customers that have been

Current Charlene's Diner exterior.

Charlene and her family.

coming here for years know that. The newer people around go to McDonald's and places like that. But it's not a diner. Diners are about the experiences. Yes, I miss the original diner, but the fact that we do a good business in the new location and the customers are happy speaks a lot to what's really important about classic diners. It's not the things or the building. A real diner is about the people and the food. I have a truck driver who comes into the diner regularly. Because he has cholesterol and sugar problems, I make him a special omelette of turkey and fresh egg whites. I want him to still enjoy his breakfast before he sets off on the road.

Charlene takes pride in how much of herself she has invested in the diner:

The reason the diner has survived is because I've always worked a lot of hours. There were many tight moments financially, but I could always roll up my sleeves, work even harder and somehow we made it through. I believe that I've always had a guardian angel looking out for me. A lot of people drive by and go to McDonald's. They pay more than they'd pay here to get food not nearly as wholesome as we make, and ours is homemade from the freshest ingredients in big portions. What I really worry about, though, is watching people get their food in drive-thrus, then they eat it in their cars in the parking lot. People need to stop, enjoy their food and rediscover conversation.

The original stool tops hang on the wall at Charlene's Diner, and the pie case is original as well. The feelings of family experienced at the original Charlene's Diner have continued at the new place, mainly because Charlene has kept the diner experience alive and well. To be sure that nothing changes in the years ahead, she has already created a succession plan that is taking place today. "I'm about to pass the diner torch to my daughter and son-in-law, and my granddaughter is already working here." However, if you ask Charlene when she'll be retiring, her response is as evasive as the manner in which she guards her recipes. "My Torpedo Sauce goes back to when I was sixteen. We put it in a grinder and also make an omelette with it. It's sort of like a sloppy joe but sweeter. It's homemade, so if you want the recipe, you'll have to buy the diner."

There are other items for which regular patrons keep coming back. "My sausage gravy is requested a lot. I serve it over chipped beef, which the younger crowd knows nothing about so they can't really appreciate it. It doesn't come out of a pouch or a wrapper. You have to try it to appreciate it." No matter what you order at Charlene's Diner, you can be assured of delicious, homemade food, but I'd draw your attention to the Hippo, so named because this unique combination of eggs, meat and cheese between two pancakes heads straight for your hips.

Norm's Diner
171 Bridge Street, Groton
1954 Silk City

John A. Espada, owner-operator of Norm's Diner, has the energy and enthusiasm of someone who's found his calling and can't wait to live it each day. Sitting under the stunning panorama of the arching spans of the Gold Star Bridge spanning the Thames River, John is like the understudy standing in the wings whose day has finally come to fill in for the ailing Broadway star. And there's never a disappointment in his performance because for all intents and purposes, John was born to be in the spotlight of the culinary stage called Norm's Diner, greeting patrons who come in for a classic diner experience. I'm reminded of *Pay as You Exit*, a 1936 Our Gang short comedy film directed by Gordon Douglas in which Alfalfa, hoping to attract customers to Spanky's barnyard production of *Romeo and Juliet*, suggests a "pay as you exit" policy: if the kids like the show, they'll pay the allotted one-cent admission on the way out. When the audience leaves, Spanky admonishes Alfalfa for his scheme. But pay they did, and Alfalfa and Spanky eat onions as a toast to their success. Although there is no actual pay-as-you-go policy at Norm's Diner, customers relish the historical diner experience, played out with John leading the show, and they celebrate the finale with great home cooking, for which they gladly pay their check knowing that the high quality of the food is well worth the fair prices.

A 1954 Silk City gem, Norm's Diner was moved to its current location in 1964 after having resided down the road near the National Submarine Memorial honoring World War II submarine veterans and the more than 3,600 submariners who lost their lives during the conflict. The largest feature of the submarine memorial on Bridge Street is the conning tower of the USS *Flasher* (SS-249). The *Flasher*, built by Groton's Electric Boat and commissioned in 1943, was credited with sinking the highest tonnage of Japanese ships (twenty-four vessels and more than 100,000 tons) during World War II. Norm's Diner still has the original tile flooring, ceiling and

Norm's Diner exterior.

Norm's Diner owner John A. Espada.

Norm's Diner Silk City plaque.

Norm's Diner interior.

stainless steel siding on the exterior. The booths and stools are also original but have been reupholstered after years of wear and tear. The back kitchen was added later.

The cast at Norm's Diner includes headliner John, who in Will Rogers fashion welcomes patrons in with menu in hand, always ready to share his perspective on life: "A diner is a tough business. There's a lot of competition, but life is about being your own shining star. Eating at a diner is a unique experience you won't find anywhere else. Can you imagine how many people have come through these doors and how many stories there are? In fact, I remember one…let me tell you about it," and the performance begins. The supporting cast includes a young cook who serves food and entertainment from his grill behind the counter as he talks with customers loud enough to be heard over his radio, the music seemingly orchestrated to his cooking prowess. The waitresses have that always-ready-to-serve attitude, with enough friendliness that makes you want to learn more about them in a good conversation.

The food at Norm's Diner is simple and simply wonderful. There's no flash or French names. It's basic diner food made and served the way it should be. "Take the pot roast. Please," Henny Youngman might have declared, but it's a meal that challenges breakfasts being the calling card of classic diners. With its accompaniment of steamed carrots and potatoes, this meal will surely please and have you coming back later in the day. And just like Youngman relied on one-liners to entertain his audience when other comedians were telling elaborate anecdotes, Norm's Diner doesn't try to outdo the competition by offering too many complicated meals. The classic creamed chipped beef is basic at its best: a huge bowl filled with shredded, dried beef covered with gravy salted to perfection. The twin patties are the foundation for Norm's double cheeseburger, which can easily become the litmus test for how a cheeseburger should taste.

Windham County

Windham County is located in the northeastern corner of Connecticut. The entire county is within the Quinebaug and Shetucket Rivers Valley National Heritage Corridor, as designated by the National Park Service. Major highways through Windham County include Interstate 395, which runs north–south from the New London County line at Plainfield to the Massachusetts state line at Thompson. The southern section of I-395 is part of the Connecticut Turnpike, which branches off the interstate in Killingly and runs east–west from I-395 exit 90, to U.S. Route 6 at the Rhode Island state line. Other north–south routes include Route 12, which parallels I-395 through many local communities, and Route 169, a National Scenic Byway traveling through rural communities from the New London County line in Canterbury to the Massachusetts state line in Woodstock. Other secondary north–south roads are Routes 89, 198, 97, 21 and 49. Major east–west routes are U.S. Route 44 from the Tolland County line at Ashford to the Rhode Island state line at Putnam and U.S. Route 6 from the Tolland County line at Windham to the Rhode Island state line at Killingly. U.S. Route 6 has short expressway segments in Windham and Killingly. Other secondary east–west roads are Routes 14, 101, 171 and 197.

The Dayville Historic District is located in the town of Killingly and was added to the National Register of Historic Places in 1988. The village of Dayville was named after Captain John Day, who owned the water privileges on the Five Mile River. With the opening of the Norwich and Worcester Railroad in 1830, Dayville became a hub for freight transport for other manufacturing villages along the river. Dayville lies in the northwestern part of the town of Killingly on the Assawaga or Five Mile River. The Norwich & Worcester Railroad has a station here and is the shipping point for several manufacturing villages around, such as Williamsville, Attawaugan, Ballouville, Elmville and Chestnut Hill. The railroad station is known as Dayville, but the post office is Killingly. The town is home to the woolen goods manufacturer Sabin L. Sayles Company, the principal industrial institution, and two churches.

ZIP'S DINER
ROUTES 12 AND 101, DAYVILLE
1954 O'MAHONY

What do Liberace, Alec Baldwin, Kim Basinger, Brian Dennehy, Renée Zellweger, Ted Williams, Joe DiMaggio and Carl Yazstremski have in common? They've all eaten at the classic Zip's Diner under the iconic neon "EAT" sign. With a reputation as gleaming as the shiny stainless steel that wraps around this wonderfully preserved place setting in diner history, Zip's is a legendary dining car, serving up the area's finest meals since 1954. Like a giant game of Twister, Zip's is centrally located between Hartford, Providence and Worcester.

The name "Zip" was the nickname of retired Connecticut state trooper Henry Zehrer, who started in the diner business in 1946 in Danielson, Connecticut. The original diner was located on Route 6 between the Powdrell and Alexander Mill and what is today the Danielson Post Office. The diner operated until 1954, when Zehrer purchased a brand-new O'Mahony diner and had it shipped up north from Elizabeth, New Jersey, to its current location. The trip from the Jerry O'Mahony Company was handled by Hoffman's Motor Transport of Belleville, New Jersey, and took two weeks due to an extended truck strike, which delayed progress in New York, compounded once they were underway again by a breakdown in Norwalk, Connecticut. One of the largest and most completely modernized diners of its time, the 101-ton behemoth made the last leg of its journey down Main Street under police escort to the cheering throngs of spectators, who were mesmerized by the forty-three-foot-long by thirty-two-and-a-half-foot-wide monolith. After a thirteen-hour process of placing the two diner

Above: Zip's Diner exterior with classic sign.

Left: Zip's Diner owner Kevin Cole.

Zip's Diner interior.

Vintage Zip's Diner postcard.

sections into the stone masonry foundation, Zip's Diner's place in diner history was a reality.

Conrad and Olive Jodoin purchased the diner from the Zehrers in 1960. Over the following years, it became a true family business with help from their children—Tom, Nancy, James and Robert—all of whom had a hand in running the business. In 1980, the second Jodoin generation took over under Tom Jodoin, with brothers Robert and James running the kitchen. Today, the diner is now on its third generation of family ownership. Kevin Cole (Nancy's son, Tom's nephew) purchased the diner from Tom in early 2010, with Robert still running the kitchen. "The neon sign on the roof and the stainless steel exterior are all original," Kevin proudly pointed out. "And the terrazzo flooring is as good as the day they poured it. The booths are all original, except they've been reupholstered. Some changes had to be made due to the age of the diner and normal wear and tear. For example, the stools were replaced because the stainless could not be repaired, and the Formica on the countertops had to be replaced. But the ceiling is original."

Zip's Diner was a haven during Hurricane Irene, a large and destructive tropical cyclone that affected much of the Caribbean and East Coast of the United States during late August 2011. Irene is ranked as the seventh-costliest hurricane in United States history, and its impact on the Dayville community is well remembered. "People who didn't leave town came to the diner in search of safety from the storm. They felt secure here. In fact, Margaret 'Maggie' Weaver made it her home throughout the hurricane."

Zip's Diner serves basic Yankee diner food. Nothing fancy or pretentious—just good, wholesome food in ample quantities to satisfy any size appetite. Breakfast is served at any time, and the assortment of offerings includes biscuits with sausage gravy, corned beef hash, steak and eggs, pancakes, French toast, omelettes, Belgian waffles—basically whatever you crave. And the coffee is always fresh. There's even a *Zippy the Pinhead* comic by Bill Griffith on the menu to distract you while your order is being prepared. Hot and cold sandwiches of all kinds are available, and dinners include such classics as Yankee pot roast, roast turkey with stuffing, baked meatloaf, chicken fried steak and New York strip, as well as pasta and seafood selections.

Although the chain stores and fast-food restaurants in the area try their best to grab the attention of prospective customers, the giant "EAT" sign that sits atop Zip's Diner is like a towering tractor beam that brings passersby into this classic roadside gem. Zip's benefits from the heavy trucking trade, as well as the nearby casino and ski resorts.

Classic Diners of Connecticut Past

One of the greatest enjoyments I get from being a motorcyclist is riding the roads of Connecticut to visit classic diners. As custom motorcycle builder Cyril Huze said regarding my public television program, DINERS, "Like burgers and ketchup, bikes and diners mix very well with each other…the joy of being on a motorcycle and finding those out-of-the-way classic eateries that invite travelers in for a home-cooked meal and friendly conversation while transporting them back in time." And for the motorcyclist, nothing is more accommodating after a long ride than a neon diner sign inviting the rider in for a good meal. For the archetypical individualistic rider, a classic diner is the only place that you go into by yourself and feel totally comfortable either eating alone or responding to the conversational invitations offered by the waitress and community of patrons.

On another layer deeper than the relationship between home-cooked food and hungry bikers, classic diners and motorcyclists share an intimate bond based on their relationship to a disappearing identity and landscape on which the very core of their being is predicated. Motorcyclists are modern-day cowboys, the two-wheeled descendants of the wranglers who tended horses to work cattle on the prairies of North America, right down to their bandanas, leather chaps, saddlebags, boots, gloves and jeans. The cowboy values of honorable behavior and mutual concern made popular by Gene Autry, Tom Mix and Roy Rogers are right at home in the code of ethics of classic diner owners. Both the modern-day motorcyclist-cowboy and the classic diner owner face a changing landscape that threatens their very existence. For the cowboy, the introduction of barbed wire to contain cattle in designated grazing areas and the building of meatpacking plants closer to railroad depots and major ranching areas collapsed the open range and reduced the need for long cattle drives, hence their skills were less in demand over time. The landscape of classic diners has analogously changed as the fast-food industry has consumed more retail space and distracted consumers away from home-cooked meals and friendly conversation to mass-produced food purchased and eaten without even having to leave one's car.

Yesterday's cowboy as epitomized in today's motorcyclist has a culture and code of ethics blended from Victorian values bordering on chivalry. A sense of self-reliance and individualism born from life on the often desolate prairie are values on which classic diner owners have built their culinary legacies. Caring for their patrons like family members, managing a business with daunting competition from corporate food chains, preparing meals as good as they would put on their own tables at home and building a meeting place for the community are synonymous with the biker code of never giving up, always being truthful, caring about others as family and respect.

For today's cowboy on his chrome horse, the diner is the modern chuck wagon, invented by Charles ("Chuck") Goodnight, a Texas rancher who introduced the concept in 1866. Goodnight modified the Studebaker wagon, a durable army-surplus wagon, to suit the needs of cowboys driving cattle from Texas to sell in New Mexico. He added a "chuck box" to the back of the wagon with drawers and shelves for storage space and a hinged lid to provide a flat cooking surface. On cattle drives, it was common for the "cookie" who ran the wagon to be second in authority only to the trail boss, not unlike the relationship between short-order cook and diner owner.

If you've frequented classic diners and let yourself experience the relationships of the patrons, the waitresses, the owner and the cook, then you can feel what the campfire was to the cowboy. Something special happens when you sit before a campfire that's similar to the experience of sitting at the counter of a crowded diner. When you embrace the warmth and companionship of the diner-as-campfire, you contact once again the past and reforge the link to those childhood memories of visiting your first diner and growing up with the values it represented. You re-experience a time when life was simple and unencumbered and true, much like nightfall on the prairie. Being at a diner is more than satiating one's hunger or dropping by for a fresh cup of coffee. The diner experience is a primal psychological necessity that connects us to those hallowed values of past generations. When we sit at the counter, we lay down the burdens of the day and embrace the moment, a lost art in today's modern world. I motorcycle and frequent classic diners because the experiences are what connect me to those values that have held true since I had my first breakfast at the College Diner in New Rochelle: hard work, loyalty, determination and community.

When I motorcycle the roads of Connecticut, I take time to pay respect to those classic diners that stand as ghosts of their once vibrant community lives. Although their hearts have stopped beating to the pulse of lively conversation, spatulas flipping burgers and waitresses shouting their special diner lingo, those that stand are stainless steel monuments to the lifeblood of entrepreneurial courage, shared optimism, independence, authenticity and heart that permeate the arteries of the classic diner experience. Just like when motorcyclists wave to one another on the open road in recognition of the sense of camaraderie implicit in their lifestyle, life in the diner is about a shared sense of community. It is in homage to the passing of classic diners that I include those that are no longer part of the active landscape of Connecticut but nonetheless retain their cherished roles as keepers of the flame.

KIMBERLY DINER
459 BOSTON POST ROAD, MILFORD
CIRCA 1961 DERAFFELE

After forty-three years at its Boston Post Road location, serving thousands of customers with delicious meals, the Kimberly Diner will close its doors in 2013. The diner, owned by New England and Connecticut Golden Gloves champion Tim Tsopanides, who was mentored by the legendary Ted "Tiger" Lowry, is going down for the count and will be purchased by the car dealership across the street. "In all the years we've been here, we were never given the opportunity to buy the property," according to Tim. "We're an institution here in Milford. So much of the community's history resides inside of the diner."

"My mom and dad came here in 1970," reflected Tim. "They bought the diner and a dream. The previous owner had named it after his daughter, but my parents never got around to changing the name. That's the way it is with diners. You get caught up in so many activities to keep the place running and taking care of the customers that something as obvious as a diner name gets back-burnered."

Kimberly Diner exterior.

It's hard to imagine this historically relevant, architecturally significant and beautifully styled space-age diner becoming a car lot. However, memories can't be bulldozed, and the role that the Kimberly Diner has played in the lives of so many residents, commuters and travelers will be remembered far above the asphalt that will soon cover this local landmark.

MILFORD DINER
13 NEW HAVEN AVENUE, MILFORD
1953 SILK CITY

It's a short motorcycle ride from the Kimberly Diner to the other side of town, where the Milford Diner, a 1946 Silk City with an attached building that predates the main structure, sits in disrepair, having been closed for years. The diner is a well-known Milford landmark, and there has been a community push to save and restore the historic structure, although the intent is to raise enough donations to convert it into a tourist and information center. Its intended

Milford Diner.

John's Diner.

prosthetic use, while at least sparing the diner from demolition, means that the diner experience will not be re-created. In fact, the nonprofit organization charged with the restoration is selling on its website everything from plates to bowls, cups, glasses and more to raise money. The "conversion to a new role" approach to restoration, while well intended, leaves my heart empty as I sit on my motorcycle, motor off, contemplating the Milford Diner when I would frequent it and take in the aromas and conversation that were its life and intent.

John's Diner
136 Connecticut Avenue (Route 1),
South Norwalk
1927 Tierney

Closed since 1995, John's Diner shows visible signs of severe neglect, both inside and out. A peek into a window reveals wood supports propping up the ceiling as assorted vegetation grows inside the long-silenced interior. There is no parking on the four-lane Connecticut Avenue and no parking lot adjacent to the diner, so I park my motorcycle down the street and walk up to pay my respects to this classic roadside icon. The humble little barrel-roof diner is the runt of the litter comprising the nearby million-dollar Silver Star Diner and the busy Post Road Diner just down the street. Even in its decomposition, John's Diner speaks to the era when U.S. 1 was the main artery through Norwalk prior to the construction of Interstate 95 and when travelers were drawn there as *the* place for a good meal and to catch up on the latest town news.

Skee's Diner
Primarily located at 589 Main Street, Torrington
Circa 1920s O'Mahony #562

Honored by being listed on the National Register of Historic Places in 2002, Skee's Diner came off the O'Mahony production line in the '20s wearing its stainless steel outer coat and its distinctive chapeau barrel roof. Adorned

Skee's Diner.

with a marble countertop, a mahogany icebox, seventeen stools and sliding entrance doors, it was shipped to its original location in Old Saybrook. It was a thing of beauty.

In 1945, local restaurateur Rudy Cielke leased Skee's Diner for ninety dollars per month in a ten-year lease and moved the diner to Torrington. Shortly after the move, Anthony Cisowski purchased the newly relocated diner in partnership with his brother, Edmund, and they officially opened for business in 1946, with Stanley "Stash" Smigel as cook. Like so many of the Connecticut diners that were hard hit by the great flood of 1955, Skee's survived the water-filled basement and continued operations. Skee's Diner went through several more owners during the ten years between 1974 and 1984. In 1987, the same year in which Skee's was sold once again, it was immortalized on a greeting card photographed by Jeffery Milstein and in a painting by John Baeder, who did a second painting of Skee's Diner in 1995. The very next year, the carousel of owners would take another turn with new owners Robert and Maria Levesque making the purchase and then leasing it in 1995, ultimately closing it down in 2001. From that time, the doors have remained shut.

In 2009, the Northwest Connecticut Chamber Education Foundation purchased the inoperative local landmark and passed it to the Torrington Historical Preservation Trust, which has relocated the diner to a warehouse and is leading the effort to restore it and then relocate it downtown, where it will be used as a welcome and information center.

Diner Lingo

Much like the secret handshake by which associates of a members-only group greet one another and acknowledge their "belongingness," diner slang has evolved from the late 1800s as a form of oral shorthand used by waitstaff to communicate their orders to the short-order cook. Similar to visiting a foreign country where English is not spoken, diner lingo is virtually unknown outside the United States. The lighthearted, tongue-in-cheek and even sometimes risqué phrases could be heard in wide use in busy diners during the 1920s, continuing on well into the 1970s. Diner lingo was never intended for use in speeding up the order-to-table process. Rather, it was a spontaneously developed mnemonic means of making orders easier to hear and remember above the conversational din of the busy diner. It also provided patrons and employees with a free form of entertainment.

While you can still hear some of the remnants of diner lingo in use today in classic diners, its prevalence has been drowned out by the emergence of fast-food chains and computer ordering. However, if you're fortunate enough to be sitting in a booth or at a counter being served by a veteran server who still speaks the diner mother tongue to audibly communicate your menu selections to the short-order cook, you may be privy to an interpersonal exchange that will take your own classic diner experience to a very special level.

#5: milk

#21: limeade

#41: lemonade

#51: hot chocolate

#55: root beer

#77: 7 Up with vanilla ice cream

#81: water

#86: take an item off the order

50-50: cup of coffee or "joe" with half-and-half

Adam and Eve on a log: two poached eggs with link sausage

Adam and Eve on a raft: two poached eggs on toast

Adam and Eve on a raft and wreck 'em: two scrambled eggs on toast

Adam's ale: water

all day: altogether

all hot: baked potato

all the way: hot wiener with mustard, meat sauce, onions and celery salt

angels on horseback: oysters rolled in bacon and served on toast

Arnold Palmer: half sweet tea, half lemonade

Atlanta: Coca-Cola (the company is based in Atlanta, Georgia)

axle grease/skid grease/cow paste: butter

B&B: bread and butter

baby juice/moo juice/cow juice/Sweet Alice: milk

baled hay: shredded wheat cereal

Battle Creek in a bowl: bowl of corn flakes cereal (the Kellogg Company is based in Battle Creek, Michigan)

beef stick: bone

belch water/balloon water: seltzer or soda water

biddy board: French toast

billiard: buttermilk

bird: chicken

birdseed: breakfast

birds in a nest: a fried egg on toast with a hole cut out of the center

black and blue: a steak cooked quickly over very high heat so that it is seared (black) on the outside and rare (blue) on the inside

black and white: chocolate soda with vanilla ice cream

black cow: chocolate milk or chocolate soda with chocolate ice cream or a soda made with chocolate ice cream and root beer

blindfolded: basted egg

blonde with sand: coffee with cream and sugar

bloodhound in the hay: a hot dog with sauerkraut

blowout patches: pancakes

BLT: bacon, lettuce and tomato sandwich

blue-plate special: a dish of meat, potato and vegetable served on a plate (usually blue) sectioned in three parts

boiled leaves: tea

bowl of red: a bowl of chili con carne

bow-wow/bun pup/tube steak/groundhog/Coney Island/Coney Island chicken/Coney Island bloodhound: hot dog

break a cowboy: western omelette

break it and shake it: add egg to a drink

breath: onion

bridge/bridge party: four of anything

Bronx vanilla/halitosis: garlic

brown bellies: baked beans

bubble dancer: dishwasher

bucket of cold mud: bowl of chocolate ice cream

bucket of hail: glass of ice

bullets/whistleberries/Saturday night: baked beans

burn it and let it swim: a float made with chocolate syrup and ice cream on top

burn one: put a hamburger on the grill

burn one, take it through the garden and pin a rose on it: hamburger with lettuce, tomato and onion

burn the British: toasted English muffin

cackleberries out west: western omelette

cackle fruit/cackleberries/hen fruit: eggs

campers: customers who "camp out" at a table, taking it up for an extended amount of time; this causes the servers to lose money because they cannot "turn the table"

canned cow: evaporated milk

cats' heads and easy diggins: biscuits and gravy

c-board: prepared to take out (in cardboard)

ceadeye: poached egg

checkerboard: waffle

check the ice: look at the pretty girl who just came in

chewed with fine breath: hamburger with onions

Chicago: pineapple sundae

chicks on a raft: eggs on toast

China: rice pudding

chokies: artichokes

chopper: a table knife

city juice: water

C.J. Boston: cream cheese and jelly

C.J. White: cream cheese and jelly on white bread

clean up the kitchen: hash

coffee dry: coffee with sugar only

coffee high: coffee with cream only (no sugar)

coffee high and dry: coffee with no cream or sugar ("black")

cops and robbers: doughnuts and coffee

cowboy coffee: coffee made with all chicory

cowboy western: a western omelette or sandwich

cowboy with spurs: western omelette with French fries

cow feed: a salad

creep: draft beer

cremate it: toast the bread

crowd: three of anything

cup o' joe/cup of mud: a cup of coffee

customer service: attractive table

customer will take a chance/clean up the kitchen/sweep the floor: hash

dish pig: dishwasher

dog and maggot: cracker and cheese

dog biscuit: a cracker

dog soup: water

don't cry over it: omit the onions

double black cow: double-thick chocolate shake

dough well done with cow to cover: buttered toast

down: on toast

drag one through Georgia: Coca-Cola with chocolate syrup

drag one through Wisconsin: serve with cheese (for example, a cheeseburger)

drag/run it through the garden: a hamburger, hotdog, sandwich or similar with all condiments (vegetables) on it

draw one/a cup of mud: cup of coffee

draw one in the dark/flowing Mississippi: black coffee

drop two: two poached eggs

drown the kids: boiled eggs

dry: a hamburger, hotdog, sandwich or similar without butter, mayonnaise or other dressing

dry stack: pancakes without butter

Dusty Miller: chocolate pudding, sprinkled with powdered malt

echo: repeat

egg o' biscuit: biscuit with egg

eggs up: two eggs fried on one side, unflipped with unbroken yolks

Eve with a lid on: apple pie (referring to the biblical Eve's tempting of Adam with an apple; the "lid" is the pie crust)

Eve with a moldy lid: apple pie with a slice of cheese

firehouse it: add chili sauce to a dish

First Lady: spareribs (based on the creation of the biblical Eve from Adam's rib)

fish eyes or cat's eyes: tapioca pudding

flop two: two fried eggs over easy

flop two, over easy: fried eggs, flipped over carefully, with the yolk very runny

flop two, over hard: fried eggs, flipped over, with the yolk solid all the way through

flop two, over medium: fried eggs, flipped over, with the yolk beginning to solidify

fly cake/roach cake: raisin cake or huckleberry pie

foreign entanglements: spaghetti

four on two over easy: two orders of eggs over easy

Frenchman's delight: pea soup

frog sticks: French fries

fry two, let the sun shine: two eggs fried on one side, unflipped with unbroken yolks that are generally runny

GAC: grilled American cheese sandwich (from the pronunciation of "GAC"; also called a "jack" or a "Jack Benny" if there's bacon on it)

GAC Tommy: grilled American cheese sandwich with tomato

gallery: booth

gentleman will take a chance: plate of hash

George Eddy: customer who didn't leave a tip

Georgia pie: peach pie

give it wings: serve it quickly

gravel train: sugar bowl

graveyard stew: milk toast (buttered toast, sprinkled with sugar and cinnamon and dropped into a bowl of warm milk)

groundhog: hot dog

guess water: soup

hail: ice

hatching it: a fried egg on toast with a hole cut out of the center

heart attack on a rack: biscuits and gravy

hemorrhage: tomato ketchup

hen fruit or hen nuts: eggs, sometimes boiled eggs

high and dry: a plain sandwich without butter, mayonnaise or lettuce

Hoboken special: pineapple soda with chocolate ice cream

hockey puck: hamburger, well done
hojack: buttered toast

hold the grass: sandwich without lettuce

hold the hail: no ice

honeymoon salad: lettuce alone

hope: oatmeal

hot balls: matzo ball soup

hot blonde in sand: coffee with cream and sugar

hot one: bowl of chili con carne

hot top: hot chocolate

hounds on an island: franks and beans

houseboat: banana split

hug one/squeeze one: glass of orange juice

ice the rice: rice pudding with ice cream

in the alley: served as a side dish

in the weeds: a waitress or cook who can't keep up with the tables or orders

Irish turkey: corned beef and cabbage

Jack Benny: grilled cheese sandwich with bacon

jawa/java/joe: coffee

Jewish round: a bagel

keep off the grass: no lettuce

ladybug: fountain man

LEO: lox, eggs and onion, usually served as an omelette (common in New York City)

let it walk/go for a walk/on wheels/give it shoes: an order to go, a takeout order

life preservers/sinkers: doughnuts

lighthouse: salt shaker

looseners: prunes

love apples: tomatoes

LTO: lettuce, tomato and onion

lumber: a toothpick

machine oil: syrup

Magoo: custard pie

maiden's delight: cherries

make it cry: with onions

Mama: marmalade

marry: consolidate food in same containers (e.g., pouring ketchup from half-filled bottles into other bottles to make full bottles)

mayo: mayonnaise

MD/Doc: a Dr. Pepper

Mike and Ike/the twins: salt and pepper shakers

million on a platter: a plate of baked beans

Mississippi mud/yellow paint: mustard

mother and child reunion: chicken and egg sandwich

mousetrap: grilled cheese sandwich

muddy moo: chocolate milk

Mully/Bossy in a bowl: beef stew

Murphy: a potato

mystery in the alley: side order of hash

nervous pudding: jello or jelly

Noah's boy: slice of ham (Ham was one of Noah's sons)

Noah's boy on bread: a ham sandwich

Noah's boy with Murphy carrying a wreath: ham and potatoes with cabbage

no cow: without milk

on a rail: fast (as in "Fries, on a rail!")

one from the Alps: a Swiss cheese sandwich

one on the city: a glass of water

on the fly: as soon as possible

on the hoof: any kind of meat, cooked rare

paint it red: put ketchup on a sandwich or dish

pair of drawers: two cups of coffee

pearl diver: dishwasher

peel it off the wall: add a leaf of lettuce

pigs in a blanket: sausages wrapped in pancakes

pin a rose on it: add onion to a dish

Pittsburgh: something burning, toasted or charred

plate o' dicks: a plate of sausages

Pope Benedict: eggs Benedict

put a hat on it: add ice cream

put out the lights and cry: an order of liver and onions

quail: Hungarian goulash

rabbit food: lettuce

radio sandwich: tuna fish sandwich ("tuna down," or tuna on toast, sounds like "turn it down," the command often repeated when the radio is on in the kitchen)

raft: toast; when used with burgers, a toasted bun

sand/gravel/yum-yum: sugar

schmeer: cream cheese, usually on a bagel

seaboard: to go

sea dust: salt

shake one in the hay: strawberry milkshake

shingle with a shimmy and a shake: buttered toast with jam or jelly

shivering hay: strawberry gelatin

shoot from the South/Atlanta special: Coca-Cola

shot out of the blue bottle: Bromo-Seltzer

slab of moo, let him chew it: rare round steak

sleigh ride special: vanilla pudding

smear: margarine or butter

spot with a twist: a cup of tea with lemon

soup jockey: waitress

splash of red noise: a bowl of tomato soup

stack of Vermont: pancakes with maple syrup

stack/short stack: order of pancakes

sun kiss/Oh Jay (OJ): orange juice

sunny-side up: eggs fried without flipping them so the yolk looks just like a sun on white background

sweep the kitchen/sweepings/clean up the kitchen: a plate of hash

the works: a hamburger, hotdog, sandwich or similar with all condiments on it

throw it in the mud: add chocolate syrup

to sell: to finish the plate

tube steak: frankfurter

twelve alive in a shell: a dozen raw oysters

two cows, make them cry: two hamburgers with onions

Vermont: maple syrup

walk a cow through the garden: hamburger with lettuce, tomato and onion

walking: to go

walking in: a new order just arriving in the kitchen
warts: olives

wax: American cheese

well-dressed diner: codfish

western coffee: coffee that has been on the range all day

we've got a gambler in the house: hash

whiskey: rye bread

whiskey down: rye toast

white cow: vanilla milkshake

why bother: decaffeinated coffee with nonfat milk

Winnie Palmer: half sweet tea, half lemonade

wreath: cabbage

wreck 'em: scrambled eggs

yellow paint: mustard

yesterday, today and forever: hash

zeppelin: sausage

zeppelins in a fog: sausages and mashed potatoes

Appendix II

Diner Recipes

Here are some traditional and updated diner specialties for you to try as you wax nostalgic about classic diners.

TOWER GRILL

TOWER GRILL HUNGARIAN GOULASH

Ingredients:

2½ pounds beef chuck, trimmed and cut in ½-inch pieces
3 tablespoons vegetable oil
1 larges onion, chopped
2 cloves garlic, minced
1 cup red wine
½ teaspoon dried basil

½ teaspoon dried oregano
1 bay leaf
2 tablespoons Hungarian paprika
½ cup tomato paste
1 quart beef broth
¼ cup Parmesan cheese, grated
¼ cup Italian parsley, finely chopped

Preparation:

1. Pat meat dry and season with salt and pepper. Heat oil on high heat in medium heavy-bottomed pot until it starts to shimmer. Add meat in small batches (to prevent oil from cooling) and sear the meat; remove and set aside.
2. Reduce heat to medium, add onions; cook until starting to soften. Add garlic; cook until onions are translucent.
3. Add wine; cook for 1 minute to evaporate alcohol.
4. Return meat to pot; add basil, oregano, bay leaf, paprika and tomato paste. Add enough beef broth to cover. Stir well and bring to boil. Reduce heat to a simmer, cover for $1\frac{1}{2}$–2 hours until meat is fork tender. Salt and pepper to taste.
5. For thicker sauce, add 1 tablespoon of cornstarch to $\frac{1}{4}$ cup of water, stir well and add to meat mixture in the last 5 minutes of cooking time.

Serve over buttered egg noodles, garnish with grated Parmesan cheese and chopped parsley.

OLYMPIA DINER

CORNED BEEF HASH

Ingredients:

3 pounds corn beef brisket	1 pound boiled Russet potatoes,
1 teaspoon mustard seeds	$\frac{1}{4}$-inch diced
1 teaspoon black peppercorns	1 pounds Spanish onion,
1 teaspoon mace	finely chopped
1 teaspoon allspice	4 tablespoons butter
2 bay leaves	salt and pepper to taste

Preparation:

1. Rinse the beef brisket under cold water and place in a large pot. Add enough water to cover the roast by 4 inches. Add mustard seeds, peppercorn, mace, allspice and bay leaves. Bring to a boil and cook for 30 minutes at a rolling boil; reduce heat to medium, resulting in a gentle boil. Cover and cook for $3\frac{1}{2}$ hours, then remove and cool.

2. Finely chop corned beef. Mix with potatoes and onion; add salt and pepper.
3. Heat butter in a large skillet; spread the corned beef hash evenly and press down with a spatula. Let it brown and then flip hash over to brown other side.

Serve as a side with fried eggs or omelette for a hearty breakfast; you could also put corned beef in your favorite omelette.

Main Street Diner

Diner Skillet

<u>Ingredients</u>:

6 eggs
3 tablespoons milk
$\frac{1}{2}$ teaspoon kosher salt
$\frac{1}{2}$ teaspoon freshly ground black pepper
$\frac{1}{4}$ cup green peppers, diced
$\frac{1}{4}$ cup onions, diced
$\frac{1}{4}$ cup cooked bacon, chopped
$\frac{1}{4}$ cup cooked sausage, chopped
$\frac{1}{2}$ cups cheddar cheese, shredded

<u>Preparation</u>:

1. Preheat oven to 350 degrees F.
2. In a medium bowl, scramble eggs with milk, salt and pepper; set aside.
3. In an ovenproof skillet over medium heat, sauté peppers and onions until tender. Add bacon and sausage until heated through.
4. Pour eggs over pepper mixture and mix together.
5. Remove from heat and top with cheddar cheese; put in oven until cheese is melted.

Serve with home fries and toast.

HOME FRIES

Ingredients:

3 Russet potatoes, boiled
3 tablespoons vegetable oil
½ teaspoon garlic powder

½ teaspoon onion powder
1 teaspoon paprika
salt and pepper to taste

Preparation:

1. Cut potatoes into bite-sized pieces.
2. Add oil to medium skillet; add potatoes and seasonings. Cook over medium heat until golden brown.

CURLEYS DINER

MOUSSAKA

Ingredients:

4 pounds eggplant (3–4 eggplants)
8 egg whites, lightly beaten
  (reserve yolks for béchamel)
2 cups plain breadcrumbs
1 pounds Russet potatoes
1½ pounds ground beef or lamb
2 large onions, finely diced
2 cloves garlic, minced
½ cup red wine
1 teaspoon ground cinnamon

¼ teaspoon ground allspice
¼ cup fresh parsley, chopped
2 tablespoons tomato paste
1 cup tomato puree
  (or crushed tomatoes)
1 teaspoon sugar
salt and pepper to taste
1 cup kefalotyri or
  Parmesan cheese grated

Bechamel Sauce
1 cup salted butter (2 sticks)
1 cup flour
4 cups milk, warmed

8 egg yolks, lightly beaten
pinch of ground nutmeg

Preparation:

Vegetables
1. Preheat oven to 400 degrees F.
2. Using a sharp vegetable peeler, partially peel eggplants, leaving strips of peel 1 inch wide around the eggplant. Slice into ½-inch slices; place slices in a colander and salt them liberally. Cover with inverted plate weighted down by heavy can or jar. Place in sink for excess moisture to be drawn out, 15–20 minutes, preferably an hour. (This process will eliminate bitterness of the eggplant.)
3. Line two baking sheets with aluminum foil and lightly grease.
4. Add splash of water to egg whites; beat lightly with a fork.
5. Place breadcrumbs on a flat plate.
6. Rinse eggplant slices and dry with paper towel.
7. Dip eggplants slices in beaten egg whites, then dredge in breadcrumbs, coating both sides. Place on baking sheets; bake for 30 minutes, turning over once during cooking.
8. When eggplant is finished cooking, remove from oven and lower temperature to 350 degrees F.
9. Peel potatoes and boil them whole until they are just done. Do not let them get soft, just cooked enough until they no longer crunch. Drain, cook and slice into ¼-inch slices. Set aside.

Meat Filling
1. Sauté ground beef (or lamb) in large pan until pink color disappears.
2. Add onion and cook until translucent, about 5 minutes. Add garlic and cook until fragrant, about 1 minute.
3. Add wine and allow to simmer; reduce. Add cinnamon, allspice, parsley, tomato paste, tomato puree (or crushed tomatoes) and sugar. Simmer uncovered, for 15 minutes, until excess liquid evaporates. Season with salt and pepper.

Béchamel Sauce
1. Melt butter in small pot over low heat. Gradually add flour to melted butter while continuously whisking to make a smooth paste. Cook for 1 minute; do not allow it to brown.
2. Add warmed milk to mixture in a steady stream, whisking continuously. Simmer over low heat until it thickens. Do not boil.
3. Remove from heat; stir in beaten egg yolks and pinch of nutmeg. Return to heat; stir until sauce thickens.

Assembly
1. Lightly grease a large, deep baking pan (lasagna pan); sprinkle bottom with breadcrumbs.
2. Leaving ¼ inch around the edges of the pan, place a layer of potatoes, top with eggplant slices.
3. Add meat sauce on top of eggplant layer; sprinkle with ¼ cup of grated cheese. Top with another layer of eggplant; sprinkle with another ¼ cup of cheese.
4. Pour béchamel sauce over the eggplant; making sure to allow sauce to fill sides and corner of the pan. Smooth béchamel with a spatula; sprinkle with remaining grated cheese.
5. Bake in a 350-degree oven for 45 minutes or until béchamel sauce is a nice golden brown color. Cool for 15–20 minutes before serving.

CHARLENE'S DINER

CHICKEN SALAD

Ingredients:

1½ pounds chicken breast	2 stalks celery, diced
1 tablespoon extra-virgin olive oil	1 tablespoon onion, minced
2 teaspoons kosher salt	1 tablespoon brown sugar
2 teaspoons freshly ground black pepper	1 cup mayonnaise

Preparation:

1. Preheat oven to 350 degrees F. Rinse chicken breasts and pat dry. Place chicken breasts in shallow baking dish, skin side up. Rub with olive oil; sprinkle both sides with 1 teaspoon each of salt and pepper. Roast 40 minutes, until juices run clear. Cool and remove skin. Shred into small pieces.
2. Add diced celery and onion to chicken; set aside.
3. Mix together brown sugar, mayonnaise and the rest of the salt and pepper; add to chicken.

Serve on lightly toasted croissant with romaine lettuce; garnish with potato chips and pickles.

COLLIN'S DINER

COLLIN'S DINER BURGERS

Ingredients:

1½ pounds Grade A ground beef
1 cup fresh parsley, chopped
1 cup onions (not sweet), finely diced
½ tablespoon black pepper
½ tablespoon salt

1 clove crushed garlic
½ tablespoon Goya adobo
  with pepper
¼ cup fresh mint, finely chopped

Preparation:

1. Knead together all ingredients until evenly mixed.
2. Form mixture into hand-sized meatballs and then pat until they are compressed into good-sized burger patties.
3. Cook to desired doneness; top with Swiss, Colby-Jack, cheddar or any combination. Add crisp bacon and any condiments you enjoy, or have it plain on a slightly grilled and buttered hard roll.

O'ROURKE'S DINER

O'ROURKE'S IRISH SODA BREAD

Ingredients:

2½ cups flour
1 cup plus 2 tablespoons sugar
½ teaspoon salt
½ teaspoon baking soda
¼ teaspoon baking powder
1 cup raisins
2 eggs, beaten

½ cup sour cream
⅓ cup vegetable oil
⅓ cup buttermilk
optional: ½ tablespoon toasted
  caraway seeds (toast in frying pan
  over medium-high heat for
  2–3 minutes or until fragrant)

Preparation:

1. Preheat oven to 350 degrees F.
2. Grease a 9x5-inch loaf pan; set aside.
3. In a medium bowl, whisk together flour, sugar, salt, baking soda, baking powder, raisins and caraway (if using). Add eggs, sour cream, oil and buttermilk; stir until just combined (do not overmix).
4. Pour dough into prepared pan. Bake until bread is golden brown on top and a knife inserted into the center comes out clean, 60–75 minutes. Let soda bread sit for at least 3 hours (up to 36 hours before using it for French toast).

Yield: 12–15 slices.

O'ROURKE'S IRISH SODA BREAD FRENCH TOAST RECIPE

Ingredients:

6 eggs
⅔ cup light cream or half-and-half
¼ cup granulated sugar
1 teaspoon vanilla extract
¼ teaspoon salt
1 loaf Irish soda bread cut into ½-inch slices
4 tablespoons unsalted butter, divided
clotted cream or whipped cream
strawberry or raspberry preserves or jam

Preparation:

1. In a large bowl, whisk together eggs, cream, sugar, vanilla and salt.
2. Dip each bread slice into egg mixture, saturating well.
3. In a large skillet, melt 2 tablespoons butter over medium heat. Working in batches, place slice in the skillet; cook until golden brown on both sides, about 4 minutes per side. Add more butter as needed.
4. Serve warm with clotted cream or whipped cream and preserves on the side.

Tony's Diner

Tony's Special Omelette

Ingredients:

3 eggs
¼ cup roasted red peppers,
    chopped
3 slices cooked bacon, crumbled
½ small onion, diced
salt and pepper to taste
2 slices cheddar (can use Swiss or American)

Preparation:

1. Mix together eggs, roasted red peppers, bacon, onion, salt and pepper.
2. Spray grill or large skillet with cooking spray.
3. Pour egg mixture onto grill or skillet; let cook until golden on bottom. Flip omelette a few times.
4. Add cheese slices on top; fold omelette in half and let sit until cheese is melted.
5. Serve with home fries and toast.

White's Diner

Chris's Gourmet Burger

Ingredients:

8 ounces ground beef
½ onion, chopped
½ green pepper, chopped
4 ounces mushrooms stem and pieces, chopped
salt and pepper to taste
shot of Tabasco

Preparation:

1. Mix all ingredients to form two hamburger patties.
2. Grill to your liking.

GREG'S MEDITERRANEAN BURGER

Ingredients:

8 ounces ground turkey
handful of fresh spinach, chopped
4 ounces feta cheese, crumbled

Preparation:

1. Mix all ingredients to form two hamburger patties.
2. Grill to your liking.

Connecticut Diner Directory by Manufacturer

There are more diners throughout Connecticut than are featured in *Classic Diners of Connecticut*. I have listed them below so that when you're traveling in the state, you can identify which ones are nearby. The author encourages readers to support local diners and keep the conversation going.

DeRaffele

Athena Diner I (1989)
3350 Post Road, Southport

Athenian Diner I (circa 1990)
1426 Whalley Avenue, New Haven

Athenian Diner II (1996)
864 Washington Avenue, Middletown

Athenian Diner III (1997)
1064 Boston Post Road, Milford

Duchess Diner (1993)
706 Campbell Avenue, West Haven

Elm Diner (1957)
111 Elm Street, West Haven

Frankie's Diner (1981)
1660 Barnum Avenue, Bridgeport

Glory Days Diner (2002)
69 East Putnam Avenue, Greenwich

Orem's (2003)
167 Danbury Road/Route 7, Wilton

Sherwood Diner (circa 1970)
901 Post Road, Westport

Shoreline Diner (1994)
345 Boston Post Road, Guilford

Three Brothers
242 White Street, Danbury

Three Brothers Diner
1038 Dixwell Avenue, Hamden

Twin Colony (circa 1988)
Routes 4 and 202, Torrington

FODERO

New Star Diner (circa 1963)
585 Lombard Street, New Haven

KULLMAN

Athena Diner II
320 Washington Avenue, North Haven

Fairfield Diner (circa 1990)
90 King's Highway, Fairfield

Silver Star Diner (1980)
210 Connecticut Avenue, Norwalk

MANNO/DERAFFELE

Blue Colony Diner (circa 1980/2003)
Church Hill Road, Newtown

MOUNTAIN VIEW

Wethersfield Diner (1951, #308)
718 Silas Deane Highway/Route 99, Wethersfield

PARAMOUNT

Triple A Diner (1970)
1209 Main Street, East Hartford

SWINGLE

New Colony Diner (1978, #478D)
2321 Main Street, Bridgeport

Penny's Diner (1984, #784DKDR)
212 East Avenue, Norwalk

WARD & DICKINSON

Trolley Stop Restaurant (circa 1930)
Route 66, Willimantic

The following were constructed on-site:

Bull's Head Diner (1993)
43 High Ridge Road, Stamford

Laurel Diner
544 Main Street South, Southbury

There are also a number of diners in Connecticut for which the manufacturers are unknown or unconfirmed. These include:

Acropolis Diner (circa 1970)
1864 Dixwell Avenue/Route 10, Hamden

Holiday Diner
123 White Street, Danbury

Parthenon Diner (circa 1980)
374 East Main Street, Branford

Penny's II Diner
2200 Black Rock Turnpike, Fairfield

Sandy Hook Diner (circa 1920)
98 Church Hill Road, Sandy Hook

Twin Pines Diner
34 Main Street, East Haven

Valley Diner
636 New Haven Avenue, Derby

Windmill Diner (circa 1968)
14 Mill Plain Road/Route 6, Danbury

Index

A

Albion, New York 27
Anthis, George 67
Anthis, Nicolas and Georgette 66
Aposporos, Maria 34
Atlanta, Georgia 28
Avenel, New Jersey 26

B

Bacder, John 132
Barnum, P.T. 55
Barriere, Wilfred H. 22, 25
Bassilakis, Aristedes "Harry" 90
Bassilakis, Harry 94
Bayonne, New Jersey 22
Bergetis, Eleni 34
Bixler Manufacturing Company 26
Bloomfield, New Jersey 26
Bloom, Joel 48
Bloom, Willy 48
Bramson Engineering Company 27
"Brass City" 72
Bridgeport 33, 51, 52, 53, 56
Buckley, T.H. 22, 25

C

Campora Dining Car Company 28
Campora, Jerry 28
Carteret, New Jersey 28
Cassidy's Diner 58, 59, 61
Cerminara, Greg and Linda 51
Charlene's Diner 113, 114, 116
Chick's Diner 114
clock tower (Waterbury) 73
Cole, Kevin 125
College Diner 128
Collin's Diner 107
Comac Inc. 27
Connecticut Flood Recovery
        Committee 62
Cotsoradis, Pete 72, 75
Cotsoradis, Steve 72, 73
Curley's Diner 33, 34, 35, 36, 38
Czako, Dan 85

D

Dayville 121, 122, 125
Delaney, Jay Eagle 59, 61
DeRaffele Manufacturing Company
        67

DeRaffele, Phil 42
Diner Group Limited 28
Diner-Mite Diners 28
diner recipes 151
Downington Diner 30
Duchess Diner 67
Dunkirk, New York 25
Dunn's Diner 101
Duprey, Philip H. 22

E

Eisenhower, Dwight D. 62
Elizabeth, New Jersey 25
Erfed Corporation 27
Espada, John A. 117

F

Fairfield County 33, 34
Fairfield, New Jersey 27
Family Diner 33, 47, 48, 49, 51
Fedkenheuer, Erwin, Sr. 27
Flint, Asa 112
Fodero Dining Car Company 26

G

Gavrilis, Emmanuel "Manny" 95
Gavrilis, Florence 95
Gavrilis, Steve and Tasos 95
Georgie's Diner 66, 67, 68, 71
Giannotti, Vincent 27
Giapoutzis, Teddy 42, 43
Groton 113, 117
Gutman, Richard J.S. 28

H

Hamzy, Mike 109
Hartford County 76
Haynes, Stearns A. 22
Hennigan, John J.E. 25
Hi Way Diner 33, 56
Holly Hill, Florida 28
Hopper, Edward 30

Hurricane Connie 62
Hurricane Diane 62

I

Irvington, New Jersey 27

J

Jack's Lunch 101
J.B. Judkins Company 23
Jewett City 113
J.G. Brill Company 26
Jodoin, Conrad and Olive 125
Jodoin, Tom 125
Joe's Diner 62
Jones, Ruel B. 21
Jones, Samuel Messer 21
Justin Time Diner 59

K

Kearny, New Jersey 28
Kullman Industries Inc. 26
Kydes, Phil 47, 48, 51

L

Librandi, Tony and Carmella 62
Litchfield County 106, 107
"Little Chef" 27
Loukoumis, Frank and Kathy 77
Lowell, Massachusetts 26
"lunch wagon king" (T.H. Buckley) 22, 25
Lycoudes, George, Gina, Anna and Maria 56

M

Main Street Diner 76, 77, 78, 79, 82
Makris Midtown Diner 82, 83
Manno Dining Car Company 27
Manno, Ralph 27
Master Diners 27
Meriden 58, 59
Merrimac, Massachusetts 23, 26

Middlesex County 100
Middlesex, New Jersey 28
Milstein, Jeffery 132
Miss Washington Diner 76, 85, 86, 89, 90
Module Mobile Inc. 28
Mountain View Diners 27
Mulholland Company 25
Mulholland Spring Company 25
Musi Dining Car Company 28, 56
Musi, Ralph 28, 56

N

Nash's Diner 62
New Britain 76, 85
New England Lunch Wagon Company 22, 25
New Haven County 58
Newington 76, 95
New London County 113, 121
New Palace Diner 59
New Rochelle, New York 22, 26
Nighthawks (Edward Hopper painting) 30
1955 flood 111
Norm's Diner 113, 117, 120
North Canaan 107
Norwalk 33, 42, 47, 122, 131
Norwalk, Ohio 26
Nowak, Eva 82

O

Oakland, New Jersey 26
Olympia Diner 76, 95, 99
O'Mahony, Jerry 22, 28, 122
Orleans Manufacturing Company 27
O'Rourke, Brian 100, 101, 102
O'Rourke, John 101
O'Rourke, John Sweeney 102
O'Rourke's Diner 100, 101, 102, 104, 105
Oyster Bay, New York 27

P

Page, Spencer G. "Pop" 101
Palmer, Charles H. 25

Papadatos, John 42
Paramount Diners 24, 26, 27
Paterson, New Jersey 26
Paterson Vehicle Company 26
Pequannock, New Jersey 27
Philadelphia, Pennsylvania 26
Plainville 76, 77, 82
Pollard Company, the 26
Post Road Diner 33, 42, 44, 45, 131
Prescott, Stephen 59

Q

Quaker Diner 76, 90, 91, 92, 94

R

Ra-Doc-a-Doodle (sandwich) 109
Ribicoff, Governor Abraham 62
Rochester Grills 27
Rochester, New York 27
Rutherford, New Jersey 27

S

Schultz, Charlene 114
Scott, Walter 21
Seymour 59, 62
Silk City Diners 26
Silver Creek, New York 25
Singac, New Jersey 27
Snide, Stanley and Lena 114
Stamford 33, 34, 35, 36, 39, 40, 41, 45
Starlite Diners 28
Sterling Diners 26
Sterling Junction, Massachusetts 25
Strand Theater 65
Streamliner model 23, 26
Svenningsen, Herluf "Curley" 34
Swingle Diners 28

T

Tangway, Jimmy 114
Tierney, Patrick J. 22
Tony's Diner 59, 62, 65, 66

V

Valentine Manufacturing Company 27

W

Ward & Dickinson 22, 25
Waterbury 58, 59, 71, 72, 73
West Hartford 76, 90, 91
West Haven 66, 67, 71
Westporter, the 66
Wethersfield 76, 82, 83
White House Cafés 22
White, Jack and Mabel 51
White's Diner 33, 51, 52, 53, 55
Wichita, Kansas 27
Windham County 121
Winsted Diner 107, 109, 112
Worcester Lunch Car and Carriage
        Manufacturing Company 22
Worcester, Massachusetts 25

Z

Zehrer, Henry 122
Zip's Diner 122, 125
Zora (Stamford artist) 45

About the Author

G arrison Leykam is recognized as a groundbreaker in reality TV as host and producer of the *Diners* television show that aired on Connecticut Public Television (CPTV). *Diners* follows Garrison and bikers chosen from open auditions who share his passions for motorcycles and diners as they ride to classic neon and chrome eateries. His theme motorcycle from the show was featured in the prestigious MotoStars: Celebrities + Motorcycles exhibit and companion coffee table book alongside bikes owned by Brad Pitt, Carlos Mencia, Keith Urban, Peter Fonda and other celebrities, as well as bands including Journey, Rush and Foreigner. He currently hosts the online radio program *Those Diner and Motorcycle Guys*, which in less than a year has garnered well over 1 million listeners. He is also author of the eBook *Eggs Over Easy Rider: My Journey from Rock & Roll Producer to Motorcycle Star and Web Radio Host*.

Garrison was profiled on ESPN2's *Extreme Magazine* TV program and recently produced and hosted a documentary called *Comic on a Half Shell*, which explored his experiences learning to become a stand-up comedian and appearing at New York City's famous Gotham Comedy Club. Garrison was a producer, engineer and A&R scout for London Records Inc. for ten years during the height of the British Wave. He produced legendary jazz pianist Erroll Garner, hit singer-songwriter Leslie Pearl and Texas band Greezy Wheels. While with London Records Inc., Garrison was also director of Recording Studio Operations, in which he worked in various capacities with the Rolling Stones, the Moody Blues, Al Green, Van Morrison, Dave Edmunds and others. A performer himself, Garrison has appeared at the legendary CBGB in New York City and the world-renowned Bluebird Café in Nashville.

Garrison talks about classic diners of Connecticut on his radio program, *Those Diner and Motorcycle Guys*. Here are some testimonials about the show from people who share his passions for diners, motorcycles and life on the road:

"I had an absolute blast doing an interview with *Those Diner and Motorcycle Guys*. They definitely did their research on me and asked some great questions covering all aspects of my life, not just my riding. Thanks for having me!"—Amber Arbucci, Victoria's Secret supermodel and wildlife photographer

"It was an absolute pleasure to be on the show. I will have trouble visiting a diner or riding ('crashing') a motorcycle without thinking of *Those Diner and Motorcycle Guys*."—Erin Ryder, Syfy's *Destination Truth* and National Geographic's *Chasing UFOs*

"It was a pleasure to chat with Garrison, an informed and enthusiastic host who really listens!"—Jon Herington, Steely Dan

"Thanks for having me on the show to discuss my passion. You set a nice, relaxed atmosphere which made it as easy as riding down the road."—Bill Dutcher, founder, Americade

"I love this show! Garrison is an awesome host, as well as a wonderful, caring person! I am so appreciative to have had the honor of being on the show… twice! Thanks! You are the best!"—Heather Sinn, world-renowned tattoo artist featured on the hit TV series *Ink Master*

"What a fun interview it was with Garrison. You obviously know your stuff about motorcycles and travel!"—Tiffany Coates, the world's foremost female motorcycle adventurer

"Garrison, thanks for having me on the show. It was a blast talking with you about our great passion of motorcycles. Your interview style made me feel right at home, like we have known each other for years. Keep the wind in your face. All the best to you, brother."—Tony Senzamici, actor, HBO series *Treme*, Starz's *Magic City*

"Thanks for having me on the show, Garrison, and for being so excited about my new TV show and my crazy life on two wheels. It was great to meet someone with your passion and enthusiasm for motorcycles but, more importantly, someone who relates to making their dreams come true. I look forward to coming back."—Neale Bayly, host of *Neale Bayly Rides: Peru* on Speed TV

"Garrison Leykam is a class act—witty, charming, insightful, engaging, funny, talented, dynamic, and he always asks the best questions. *Those Diner and Motorcycle Guys* are a sure hit!"—Cat McLean, singer, songwriter, guitarist, keyboardist, cellist and producer

"What's more fun than BS'ing about motorcycles with a couple of guys who are just as fanatical about them as I am? Well, doing it at the diner would be!"—Lance Oliver, author, *The Ride So Far*

"*Those Diner and Motorcycle Guys* remains one of the freshest interviews I have done on my book tour. Who knew that a book on weight and life could intersect so well with the world of diners and bikers. Garrison's energy is infectious and reminds us all that mindfulness lurks everywhere—on a bike, at a table, in a diner. Great radio show that reminds us all to find the pleasure in the moments and that we have a lot more in common than we think!"—Dr. Ramani Durvasula, author, *You Are WHY You Eat* (*Dr. Oz*, Dr. Drew's *Lifechangers*, *The Today Show*)

"The interview was great, professional and easygoing. David Letterman better watch it; these guys can take his show over."—Mike Werner, internationally renowned motorcycle and travel journalist and photographer

"Thank you so much for interviewing me. Garrison, you are a terrific interviewer, and it was a pleasure being on your show. I appreciate your generous spirit."—Alexandra Paul, *Baywatch* TV star, actress, athlete and activist

"[Garrison] was very well prepared and asked great questions. It was a most pleasant experience, and the time was over before I knew it."—Dr. Charles M. Falco, experimental physicist and curator of the Solomon R. Guggenheim Museum's The Art of the Motorcycle exhibit

"Thank you very much for having me on your show. You really have terrific questions, and you clearly do your homework. I am going to be a regular listener!"—Christina Shook, photographer and author of *Chicks on Bikes*

"*Those Diner and Motorcycle Guys* were so much fun! I had a great time speaking with Garrison and Ralph—they made me laugh and feel really comfortable."—Elisabetta Canalis, supermodel, actress and PETA activist

"Garrison is without a doubt the best at what he does."—Ron Eckerman, manager for the Doors and author of *Turn It Up!*

"I had the honor of being interviewed by the illuminating, coruscating, auroral Garrison. His cognition to blend comedy with drama in his questions was so refreshing. He knew more about me than I do! Never has an interviewer made me feel more comfortable. My respect for him is immeasurable."—Laurene Landon, actress, *Airplane II*; *I, the Jury*; *All the Marbles*; *Hundra*; and *Maniac Cop*

"Garrison is like a biker buddy you've ridden with for years. It was great fun to hang out and swap stories from the road with him."—Paul James, director of consumer influence and product communications, Harley-Davidson

"What could be finer than a show that celebrates two of the best things ever given to the world by America…diners and motorcycles."—Christine Ohlman, Saturday Night Live Band

"*Those Diner and Motorcycle Guys* 'get it.' The only thing I missed was a cup of coffee and a nice piece of blueberry pie."—Tom Cotter, author, *Harley in the Garage*

"Garrison and Ralph aren't simply radio hosts; they are the guys riding down the road with you and meeting you across town for a bite to eat. They are the final authority on bikes and diners."—Joel Rabb, Chicago-based attorney and motorcycle rights advocate

"Food, bikes and music…what more is there?"—Carl Verheyen, Supertramp